WORLD RESOURCES AND PEACE

WORLD RESOURCES
AND PEACE

LECTURES DELIVERED UNDER THE AUSPICES OF
THE COMMITTEE ON INTERNATIONAL RELATIONS
ON THE BERKELEY CAMPUS OF THE
UNIVERSITY OF CALIFORNIA
1939

UNIVERSITY OF CALIFORNIA PRESS
BERKELEY AND LOS ANGELES
1941

UNIVERSITY OF CALIFORNIA PRESS
BERKELEY, CALIFORNIA

———

CAMBRIDGE UNIVERSITY PRESS
LONDON, ENGLAND

CONTENTS

THE NATURAL ENDOWMENT OF THE NATIONS: THE DISTRIBUTION OF POPULATION AND RESOURCES

———

JAN O. M. BROEK

ASSOCIATE PROFESSOR OF GEOGRAPHY
IN THE UNIVERSITY OF CALIFORNIA

Lecture delivered October 3, 1939

THE NATURAL ENDOWMENT OF
THE NATIONS: THE DISTRIBUTION
OF POPULATION AND RESOURCES

THE FIRST lecture of the series serves an introductory purpose. The subject is very broad and thus it is clear that
a world-wide and accurate survey would require more time
than is now available. I have selected a theme that seems especially vital to an understanding of the present world situation.

I wish to stress the word "understanding." It is my purpose
to leave my personal judgment of right and wrong as much
as possible out of this lecture. As a matter of fact, some of the
things I will say are adverse to my emotional leanings. But
we can at least try to think objectively.

The present conflict in Europe is certain to have reverbera-
tions over the entire world. I believe, therefore, that we are
justified in concentrating on the background of certain European problems. I do not wish to go into great detail, nor offer
any specific solutions. Rather, I would put before you some
general observations; essentially, they concern the changing
relations between peoples and physical resources and the resulting economic and political shifts.

By physical resources I mean those elements of the natural
environment that have utility for man. It is obvious that this
appraisal varies, depending upon the stage of civilization: a
plant, an animal, a mineral which may not have had the
slightest value for a primitive society may for our modern
Western civilization be of the greatest significance.

It is this dynamic nature of the interplay between man and the land that explains why regions shift in economic value and often also in political strength. Each period of history has had its areas which were particularly favored by the dominant resource pattern. For example, the oases of Egypt and Mesopotamia, the Mediterranean, or the Atlantic margins of Europe and North America, each in turn became zones of economic energy, accumulating wealth and political power.

With the evolution of material civilization, man not only came to use more and more elements of his direct natural environment; he also became increasingly dependent upon commodities from other regions. Though the facts are obvious and hardly need supporting evidence, I should like to quote some examples from the field of mineral resources; it is in this field particularly that changes in evaluation of areas have been precipitous, in response to new technical uses of metals. Formerly, if a nation had coal and iron in large quantities it had the prerequisites for industrial development, provided its peoples had the science, technical skill, and capital. Today, a great many other minerals are just as vital to a modern nation. Ideally speaking, the lack of such minerals should not be a hindrance, because the exchange of goods and services can take care of this. We cannot ignore the reality, however, which shows that (for whatever reasons) ownership or effective political control is considered a great advantage.

Even so short a period as that lying between the beginning of the first World War and the present conflict shows some striking changes in production centers. For instance, we may consider petroleum, bauxite (which is the aluminum-bearing ore, copper, and chromium (one of the metals used for making steel alloys, especially stainless steel).

In 1913 the greatest producer of crude oil was the United States, followed by Russia with about one-fourth the United States production, then by Mexico, Rumania, and Netherlands East India. In response to the ever-increasing use of petroleum products for automobiles, airplanes, and ships, and for the lubrication of machinery, the world production is today over five times as large. The United States still has its dominant position, but Venezuela now contends with Russia for second place, and Iran (Persia) is fourth, followed by Netherlands East India, Rumania, and finally Mexico. The new fields in Arabia and Baluchistan may upset this list.

Aluminum has become increasingly important, especially as a weight-saving material in transportation, and also for transmission cables and other purposes. For bauxite in 1913 the world was practically dependent upon France and the United States. Today France still is the largest producer, but now Hungary takes second place, and the other important countries exporting bauxite are Yugoslavia and Italy in Europe, British and Dutch Guiana in South America, and Netherlands East India.

As to copper, in 1913 the United States was the outstanding producer, with more than seven times the amount from the next on the list, Japan. At present the United States still is first, but it mines less than one-third of the world total. Chile and Canada in the Western Hemisphere, northern Rhodesia and the adjacent Belgian Congo in Africa, in the order named now produce together almost half of the world's copper.

Chromium was of little consequence twenty-five years ago. In 1913 the prominent chrome-ore producers were British southern Rhodesia and French New Caledonia in the southwest Pacific. Today Russia heads the list, followed by southern Rhodesia, the Union of South Africa, and Turkey, which together supply more than three-fourths of the world's total.

These examples show clearly the nature of the shifts in areas of strategic importance and demonstrate strikingly how the older European industrial countries have become more and more dependent upon other regions for the modern minerals.

Now let us turn from physical resources to the people. Here, too, we find significant changes in terms of time and space. We must, however, stretch our period of comparison to gain a true perspective. The outstanding fact of modern history is the expansion of the peoples of European stock, associated with the emergence of technological civilization. Though population data are notoriously unreliable for former centuries, and even today are far from complete, enough research has been done to justify some rough estimates.

We may take as a point of comparison the middle of the 18th century, when the European expansion was on its way but was as yet unaided by modern technology. The world population in 1750 was roughly 660 millions; at present it is some 2000 millions—three times as much. It was especially the peoples of European stock that caused this increase. In 1750 they formed slightly more than one-fifth of the world's population; today, of a far larger world total, one-third. In Europe the population grew from 140 to 500 millions, which is three and one-half times as much as it was two centuries ago. Besides this, there are now outside of Europe some 160 million people of pure European stock. The other peoples have, in general, also increased, but none so fast as the Europeans. Asia, which makes the best showing, seems to have had some 400 million inhabitants in 1750 and now has about 1000 millions, or two and one-half times as much.

It is well known that this rapid increase of European peoples is now coming to an end. As a matter of fact, some nations are already on the verge of a decline of population. The great push of the white man into various parts of the world draws to a close. One may even go further and say that in some parts of the world the white man is already on the defensive. This is, of course, not purely a matter of numbers, but just as much, or more, the result of other races' borrowing from the West the tools and techniques which once were its monopoly. This countermove is most noticeable in eastern Asia, and one can have little doubt that it will spread to other areas. Naturally it will be the colonial powers, those which were most active in the European expansion, that will have to bear the brunt of this coming conflict.

From resources and peoples we turn to their product, the nation. A nation is a union between a people and its habitat. The land influences the people, the people change the land. A nation is a spiritual community of people, but such a community can maintain itself only if built upon a strong material foundation. It is difficult to say what is the most essential element in forming a nation. On the spiritual side, language, as the main vehicle of thought, is doubtless a strong factor, but it is not always decisive, as many exceptions show. (United States—England; South America—Spain, or Portugal; Belgium or Switzerland—France.) Race or religion may have their influence, but they are usually of minor importance. The French historian Renan once defined a nation as "a large community based on a consciousness of sacrifices made for the common weal in the past and on a tacit agreement to stand together in the future in this same spirit of loyal collaboration.... In this sense," he remarks, "the existence of a nation is a plebiscite continued from day to day." The value of the definition lies in its stress on the spiritual ties as born from a common history, without emphasis upon any single factor. Of course, these spiritual ties must be taken to include the economic common interest, which, in my opinion, has played an important role in the formation of nations. (For example, the divorce of the Low Countries from the German Empire, mainly because of differing economic interests; the formation of national cores in Flanders and Holland, and the development of their own language and culture.)

Each nation has its nucleus from where its power emanates; usually this is the cradle of national consciousness where its traditions and customs were formed. If there are no physical barriers, like the ocean, the limits of a nation are often ill defined, and political boundaries may cut through a no man's land of fluctuating loyalties. It is particularly in the transition zones between different culture areas that this continual plebiscite takes place. Here groups are apt to shift allegiance from one side to the other, depending on where the attraction—or pressure—is strongest, and the national sphere expands or contracts accordingly. If I may use the terminology of the geologist, such areas may be compared to fault zones between the more stable blocks on either side. Sometimes in this borderland separate national entities may crystallize, and thus the shatter belt may become stabilized. We have a good example of this in the region between Romance (Latin) and Germanic cultures where we find the strip of independent states: The Netherlands, Belgium, Luxemburg, and Switzerland.

But in eastern Europe, on the margins of the former Russian, Turkish, German, and Austrian empires, from Baltic to Mediterranean, lies another fault zone—a fault zone still quite active. Here the crosscurrents of migrations have deposited a conglomerate of races, languages, and religion groups, and economic and social castes. There is constant strife between the various factions, and oppression of minorities by the national groups in power. So far, strong harmonious nations have not developed here; at present the region can only be characterized as being socially and politically immature. In my judgment, the continuation of this diversity is mainly due to economic conditions, a point to which I shall return later.

Now let us look at Europe as a whole, to see how these ideas of nations and of resources can be applied. I may start with a simple observation: if we look at a political world map, we see how the lion's share of the overseas colonies, protectorates, or other dependencies is in the hands of oceanic Europe, from Great Britain to Spain. This reveals a basic contrast in development between the Atlantic seaboard and the continental part of Europe.

Before the so-called "Industrial Revolution," water transportation was the only efficient means of moving goods in bulk beyond short distances. A people on the coast had its front door on the world's highway. The merchant cities of Venice and Genoa at one time dominated the Mediterranean; the Hanse merchants of the Baltic had their golden age; but no peoples gained such a wide sweep of trade and possibilities of conquest as those living on the shores of the Atlantic. Beginning with the great discoveries, this zone became a region of bustling economic activity; it had stimulating relations with all parts of the world; it accumulated wealth and power. In comparison, the rest of Europe was like a scattering of rustic peasant communities, mere provinces to the metropolis. Agriculture remained the mainstay of continental Europe, and local squabbles its main worry.

There is a close relationship between the rise of economic power in this oceanic zone and the development of strongly welded national states. Though other factors have played their part, there is no denying the correlation between the two phenomena: national units developed because some vital common interest transcended the conflicts of local groups, and in turn the powerful states tied the people closely together.

The idea of the nation and national state spread to other parts of Europe; as a matter of fact, here (as for instance, in Germany) the concept often was more ably expressed just because the lack of national unity was more keenly felt than in the seaboard nations to whom it had come almost as a matter of course. But without a broad material base the national states of central Europe would have remained an idle dream.

It was toward 1800 that the so-called "Industrial Revolution" began to change our civilization. The term is incorrect in many respects, especially because new resources, functions, and forms are still being added, and the machine civilization is still spreading over the earth.

With this new technology an entirely different set of factors began to operate. New means of communication and transportation diminished the former handicaps of the continental areas, as compared to the maritime countries. New resources, especially minerals, such as coal, iron, and later copper, aluminum, nickel, manganese, and oil, became of vital consequence. In short, the new technology revolutionized the appraisal of regions with respect to their material value and their strategic location.

We may turn a moment to the United States in order to realize fully the significance of this new complex of forces. This country was particularly fortunate in that its expansion took place during the period of rising technology. Perhaps it is more correct to say that the machine civilization made possible this expansion and consolidation of a nation of continental proportions. Anyway, the point is that this country was shaped in harmony with the new technical-economic forces. If America stands powerful in the world of today, and if it may hope for a still greater tomorrow, it is because it fits perfectly into this modern resource pattern.

Now let us consider Europe. Whatever the historical processes were that determined the political boundaries of Europe, they had, until recently, nothing to do with the subsoil or with the modern means of communication. Even as late as 1870 Germany took Alsace-Lorraine from France principally for strategic reasons; today, though this function is still useful, the greatest value of the region lies in its iron deposits, a rich resource only after a technique had been developed (in the 1880's) to extract the phosphorus from these ores. Briefly, it is almost pure luck if a state has many or none of the minerals that today spell power or weakness.

New means of transportation have, of course, benefited all nations. But there is no denying that they have emancipated the landlocked regions. The railroad made possible the long-distance moving of bulky goods overland; the automobile and truck have served to complete the network; the aeroplane has added the atmosphere as a medium of transportation—a medium that lies over both land and water. Even now, while this new means of transport is only beginning to be developed, its tremendous significance has already become obvious. In a strategic sense, it has seriously diminished England's advantage in its island position: it has strengthened a semicontinental nation, like Germany, which can strike alike to east and west, over land and water.

Pointing out these changes in resources and in transportation is not prophesying any definite political changes, nor recommending a fatalistic attitude. It is recognizing that there are economic forces at work that diminish the superiority once enjoyed by the oceanic wing of Europe. It means the emergence of new areas of economic importance. Whether the potential political power will be transformed into kinetic energy will depend on many other factors.

The strategic nations in this emergence of continental Europe are Germany, Russia, and the shatter belt of peoples between them. I will attempt to sketch here in a few words some vital features of their resource structure. Russia as a continental power is the absolute European antithesis of maritime England. Its expansion from the Baltic and the Black Sea to the Pacific has been a territorial conquest. For all practical purposes it has always been a landlocked (or icelocked) state, reaching the open ocean of the Pacific only at its extreme eastern end, far away from the nation's core. It remained a feudal country of peasants and landed gentry until within the present century. Although certain beginnings were made before 1900, it is only in the most recent decades that the country has come to grips with the Industrial Revolution.

Considering the youth of technological Russia, we may commend the progress made; but this should not be exaggerated in picturing the present U.S.S.R. as an industrial giant. In comparison with other industrial countries, Russia is still preponderantly agricultural and with a low standard of living. In this connection we might in passing note another contrast to England. England could finance her industrial investments from capital earned in the preceding commercial epoch. Soviet Russia must finance her industrial construction mainly from what savings (or sacrifices) the internal economy offers.

But if Russia is today still in a transitional stage—and the human factor in future development is unpredictable—it doubtless has the physical resources for a vast expansion of the modern type of economy. Its subsoil contains a greater variety of important minerals than any country except the United States. This is a very favorable position, in view of the tend-

ency toward self-sufficiency, and in view of the fact that it has
a serious lack of funds with which to purchase raw materials
in competitive markets. Russia is a real "have" nation in contrast to Germany, its new "friend" and neighbor (if these
terms are not mutually exclusive in this friction zone).

The U.S.S.R. is more than self-sufficient in the production
of such staple commodities as lumber, wood pulp, grains, coal,
petroleum, iron, manganese, and chromium, and perhaps will
be so for copper and nickel. In view of the large output, it is
surprising to find in the trade statistics relatively small exports
of these goods. Only lumber is a large item; several of the
other commodities, such as oil and chromium, have even declined in their export in the most recent years. It is tempting
to guess at the reasons for this phenomenon and to speculate
how far Russia is actually able or willing to supply Germany
with raw materials, but such speculation would lead to a de-
tailed discussion of current events, which is outside the purpose of this lecture.

Germany is intermediate in structure between Britain and
Russia. It is the outstanding example of a major industrial
country that has very few of the raw materials it manufactures. Only coal and potash are abundantly available in Germany. Having lost the iron mines of Lorraine and of part of
Silesia after the first World War, she must import more than
half of her iron-ore supplies. For all other metals and oil
Germany must import from 60 to 100 per cent of its consump-
tion. Besides the minerals, there are huge deficits in lumber,
pulpwood, wool, and oils and fats, not to speak of the obvious
lack of commodities which specifically come from the sub-

tropics and tropics, as for example cotton, rubber, and such pleasant luxuries as coffee. In a normal economy all these goods were paid for by the impressive exports of processed metals, machinery, chemical products, and other merchandise. The annexations of recent years have added a few mineral deposits, it is true, but this is largely offset by the greater imports necessary to continue the industries of the Czech country and Austria. The highly developed German chemical industry has been able to find numerous substitutes, but most of them are as yet more expensive and less satisfactory than the goods they must replace. Besides, the substitutes finally depend again on other raw materials and on the building of machinery to make them, which in turn means a new demand for metal and labor.

The wish to control sources of needed raw materials is not new. The German foreign policy before the first World War had Janus faces: one looked toward the ocean and an overseas colonial empire, while the other looked toward the East for continental expansion. The German navy and the projected Berlin-Bagdad railway were symbols as well as instruments of this dual policy. Nazi Germany has concentrated on a drive to the east. We will not speculate here whether this means that it has given up its demand for colonies or whether it will ask for them as soon as, or if, its plans for the east succeed. For the time being, at least, the continental expansion stands in the center of Germany's interest.

Before the World War, technical and industrial Europe reached east as far as the line Danzig, Silesia, over Vienna, to Trieste at the northern end of the Adriatic. In the most recent decades, Russia has been building up its machine civilization. In between lies the zone that is now becoming an anomaly in Europe, a zone overwhelmingly agricultural in economy and almost feudal in its social structure, a crazyquilt of culture, language, race, and religion groups. Since this region lacks the financial and technical equipment for autonomous internal development, some outside power is bound to take control and manage the peoples as well as the resources.

In my personal opinion, the happiest solution for the peoples concerned would have been a development with the help of western European capital and technology, since it would have left them considerable latitude in matters of a national-political nature. Unfortunately, however, the Atlantic seaboard nations have never shown great economic interest in this belt, and quite naturally so, for their colonies, and such young sovereign states as the United States and Argentina, promised much safer investments and quicker profits than eastern Europe. Postwar support was born of the political desire to set up a cordon of buffer states, directed against Germany as well as Russia; and most of the loans made to the new vassal states were intended to strengthen their military value. Such exploitation as that of the oil fields of Rumania and of various mineral deposits in the Balkans has been of an extractive nature and the social-economic benefits to the native population are quite limited. Besides, the nations of oceanic Europe have little need for the agricultural products of southeastern Europe. France, with her North African resources, is almost self-sufficient in grains; England gets her food supply from the Dominions, Denmark, Holland, and the small Baltic states.

On the other hand, the markets of central Europe are not only closer to the Balkan countries and to Poland, but also more complementary in character. Germany and the former Austria and Czechoslovakia need the agricultural and mineral raw materials, while eastern Europe needs manufactured articles. The trade statistics prove the existence of this mutual relationship. Were it not for the constant and all too well justified fear of political domination following economic penetration, all parties concerned could only welcome this form of coöperation.

It is extremely difficult to look away from the present misery—and from that which is sure to come—and evaluate coolly the historical process. But it seems quite possible that eventually the political domination will further the economic development of the subjected peoples. As means of transportation and communication are extended, industrial equipment installed, and agricultural methods improved, they may for a time mainly serve the dominant power, but in the long run they will strengthen the economic structure and tend to reduce petty differences. And this process may be relatively rapid: the invader is not dealing here with primitive groups, such as the British found in most of their colonies, but with old European peoples who by geographic and historic circumstances have been left behind in the rush for economic and political power and who lack the national unity and relative prosperity that is part of the complex.

I will leave open the question of which power, Germany or Russia, is the more acceptable, or less objectionable, to the peoples concerned. It cannot be economic necessity that drives

Russia to territorial expansion. But it is vital to Germany—in her own view—to gain control over the larger part of south-eastern Europe, now that she has apparently lost all hope of expanding farther toward the east. The Balkans have a surplus of grains, animal products, olive oil, tobacco, and fruits; they have many metals, such as iron, copper, lead, zinc, and chromium, and especially attractive are the large deposits of aluminum ore. The oil of Rumania is another objective; however, one should note that the reserves here are apparently small.

If the Berlin-Bagdad line is more than a forgotten dream, one may speculate on the vistas which the oil fields of Mesopotamia and Persia and even the newly opened ones of Arabia offer to the German desire for expansion. But not only would Germany touch here on a vital link in the British Empire; the farther she should push to the southeast, the longer would be the flank she exposed to Russia. For a time, some form of cooperation between Germany and Russia may seem possible, but essentially the two are contending powers in their continental interests.

Let us summarize these observations. Before the Industrial Revolution the expansion of European peoples and the building up of colonial empires radiated from the Atlantic seaboard, where wealth accumulated and powerful national states developed. The Industrial Revolution brought a new set of forces into play which tended to offset the former handicaps of the continental areas. The new civilization spread to central Europe, then to Russia, jumping the shatter belt in between. Now this "third Europe" is in a stage of transition to the new phase. Various circumstances have prevented western Europe from taking an active part in this development, and it seems probable—whether one likes it or not—that Germany or Russia will take over the leadership in this zone. Germany needs this zone, certainly its southern half, more than Russia does, but it faces immense difficulties for any sustained dominance. The U.S.S.R., comparable to the United States in its broad territorial base and its wealth in minerals, may well, in time, become the real power of continental Eurasia.

We have seen how the boundaries of the European states are in the main based on the national criterion. These boundaries, as was pointed out, have little or no relation to present economic conditions—a discrepancy that will be further accentuated as time goes on. This is the dilemma of Europe: on the one hand, the wish for sovereign national states; on the other, the need of physical resources as a basis for material existence.

The cultural significance of a national life is not to be disputed, but it appears that the national idea has overreached itself. Is it not possible to save the spiritual values and at the same time provide a wider and more secure material foundation?

To answer this question we must remember that the idea of the national state is a relatively recent one. Being a historical concept, it may in time loose its grip again. This does not mean that Europe is likely to become a standardized, uniform civilization. Rather do I expect, or at least hope, that it will be possible to restrict the national spirit to its true function of cultural expression, in other words, to divest it of its power to make national boundaries into economic barriers. In short, the only solution is cultural autonomy for the different groups, with economic unity for the whole.

If we look at present-day Europe, it seems almost preposterous to express this hope. And yet, exhaustion following a long war, or fear for the rising eastern giant Russia, might well bring about what peace could never realize.

But whatever the solution, if Europe is to be saved from complete destruction, there must be established a new order: one different from that imposed at Versailles twenty years ago, and different from that dictated from Berchtesgaden today.

THE PROBLEM OF
THE UNSATIATED STATES

———

FRANKLIN C. PALM
PROFESSOR OF MODERN EUROPEAN HISTORY
IN THE UNIVERSITY OF CALIFORNIA

Lecture delivered October 10, 1939

THE PROBLEM OF
THE UNSATIATED STATES

THE HELLHOUNDS of war have been unleashed on the European continent for the second time in a quarter of a century. For the past eight years their growls have mounted in a warning crescendo, but the well-fed states refused to heed the ominous sounds until it was too late.

Over the face of Europe millions remembered the searing pain and suffering of four fateful years and their immediate aftermath... and they were revolted. Their rulers gave reassurances that they understood. A tall, elderly man with an umbrella told the world, in tones of heartfelt sincerity, "I am a man of peace." A portly, barrel-chested Frenchman, between terse and pointed allusions to *La Belle Patrie,* voiced the desire of his forty million compatriots for its corollary *La Belle Paix;* while on the eastern side of the Rhine a little man with a mustache was somehow convincing his listeners—between "Sieg Heils!"—that the Big Stick he was brandishing was really an olive branch. Far to the north, in a building surrounded by massive walls which shone pink in the sunlight over the steppes, sat a chunky hulk of a man, pulling at his big mustache with one hand and holding a pipe in the other. And he just sat and pulled at his pipe and then at his mustache—and didn't say a word.

And yet today three of the greatest powers of Europe are plunged into a conflict which may well prove the Armageddon of Western civilization. Everywhere people voice the eternal query: "Why? Why?" That question has been answered by the philosophers over and over again. Hate, envy, greed, fear, suspicion—these are the whys of the present struggle. It is the historian's task, however, to demonstrate not only why, but also how this blight on humanity has come about.

It was Bismarck who first made the distinction between the "satiated" and the "unsatiated" states. The essence of his dictum is that at any given period of time "the existing equilibrium, the prevailing distribution of powers, the established ratios of territories, populations, armies, navies, colonies, etc., will appear ideal to the States which are its beneficiaries and unendurable to the States which do not feel that they have received their just due." The satiated powers are usually the victors, and the unsatiated states the vanquished, in the most recent war. There are necessary qualifications to such a generalization, however, since the interests of some states are too complex—and even contradictory—to permit the unalterable placing of them in one or the other category. Italy and Great Britain are examples.

I have implied that this problem of the unsatiated versus the satiated states is not necessarily a postwar one. As a matter of fact, the broader currents of European power politics have always, with few exceptions, expressed themselves in these terms. As a result of the defeat of France in the Franco-Prussian War of 1871, that nation was changed from a satiated state to an unsatiated power. Satiation meant the recovery of Alsace-Lorraine. The German Empire, satisfied with the status quo created after 1871, was a satiated power. Great Britain, a satiated state, went to war in 1914, not for revision as did the French, but to eliminate the menace of imperial

German sea power and German competition in the market-places of the world.

Thus the struggle for power goes on without ever really stopping. The equilibrium is never satisfactory to all countries, since the peace treaties which establish it are rarely dictated in the interests of all. The victorious nations impose conditions on the vanquished which automatically produce a revisionist sentiment among the latter. Any attempt by the unsatiated—short of war—to compel a change in the status quo sets up a defense reaction on the part of the satiated in the form of counteralliances and armaments, which increases the precariousness of the equilibrium. Each new step of the "have nots" to redress the balance of power is met with compensatory policies by the "haves" until the breaking point is reached. And the satiated powers consistently balk at changing the status quo in the interest of justice for all until it is too late. In such a situation, a Sarajevo or a Danzig merely marks the point beyond which the gamblers in international power politics are willing or able to go.

Since the end of the first World War, certain nations have been unsatisfied with the political, territorial, and economic status quo created by the peace treaties. They have repeatedly asked—and sometimes have demanded—certain changes in the newly established order, but, as they explain it, they have been unable to obtain the proper consideration of their demands. In retaliation, they have during the past few years deliberately built up their military forces to bring about changes by threats—or, if necessary, by recourse to arms.

Opposition to the status quo came chiefly from three nations—Japan, Italy, and Germany. Exponents of the post-World War settlements were France, Great Britain, and the United States. The former three demanded a new deal; the latter three stood pat against changes. Great Britain and France, to believe their spokesmen, are today fighting to defend their just rights as delineated by the terms of the Versailles treaty—terms, let it not be forgotten, which were imposed upon German statesmen who were not consulted, but bluntly told to sign or else.

The conflict between the two blocs of powers has, of course, lent itself to glib clichés, some of which find very little justification in the factual details of the situation. One section of opinion regards the present issue as a struggle between Democracy and Statism; a few maintain that it represents the rivalry of finance capitalism and barter; others call it, in a most categorical fashion, the battle of the "haves" (the satiated states) and the "have nots" (the unsatiated states). Our discussion will deal for the most part with this last-named view, in an attempt to investigate its historical validity.

But just what is this problem of the unsatiated states? Many people find the answer to the question comparatively simple. They maintain that the governments of the unsatiated states want nothing less than world supremacy. While the desire for power on the part of these countries originally might have been only a means to enable a state to improve the condition of its people, by now it is, in Germany especially, an end in itself. Therefore, they say, Hitlerism must be overthrown.

To the contrary, another interpretation of the "have" versus the "have not" theory is that the demands for changes in the status quo—demands which brought about the present struggle—arose from conditions of actual need. Exponents of this belief maintain that the origins of the war lay in the resolve of the satiated powers to keep what they had and the determination of the unsatiated states to get those things which they needed.

What did these unsatiated nations want? More land and colonies for increasing populations; more raw materials for expanding industries; and more markets for their increasing industries—these were the fundamental demands of the "have not" powers. According to them, the world has been parceled out and the best portions were already occupied when they became modern industrial nations. Consequently, pressure of population, lack of necessary raw materials, and increasing need of markets to dispose of their manufactured goods had forced them to demand territorial changes in order to meet the requirements of a higher standard of living for their people. At all times these governments insisted that they did not want war, but that they were prepared to take risks to attain their ends.

It is not difficult to evaluate the claims of these dissatisfied states. Consider first their need for food. In Japan there were, in 1937, 2418 people for every square mile of arable land, compared with only 100 in the United States. Consequently, it was impossible for Japan to produce enough food within her borders to supply her people with a healthy and adequate diet. Italy and Germany, to a lesser degree, also wanted more land to supply the needs of their citizens. These were not the only countries that had similar desires. Belgium, Holland, China, and India all suffered from lack of fertile land; but they have not been so loud in their protests.

This problem of providing food for a nation of people, however, must be considered in relation to the increase in population. In the United States, England, and France, where the populations were nearly stationary, governments had enough foodstuffs at home or in their colonies to provide for their people. But in Japan and in Italy, where the populations were increasing rapidly, there was a real need of finding employment, and thus food, for the citizens. These people could not obtain pieces of land; and, without raw materials and markets, industries could not expand and thus labor could not be fully absorbed by industry.

In Germany the problem of inequalities in land and population was not so critical. While Hitler, by conquest and by his program to encourage births "to strengthen the German race," increased the population of Germany, it was difficult, prior to the war, to prove that on a war-economy basis Germany was suffering acutely from overpopulation. As a matter of fact, Great Britain was more densely populated than Germany, Japan, or Italy. But England had solved her problem through industry and trade, especially with her empire.

Unfortunately, the unsatiated powers were unable to solve their problems of inadequate foodstuffs and overpopulation by industrialization and trade—manufacturing goods which could be exchanged for food. Germany, Italy, and Japan lacked raw materials. Of the important essentials, coal, tin, copper, petroleum, rubber, potash, and cotton, Germany had a sufficient supply of only two: coal and potash. Even so, she was better off than Italy, for the latter had almost no coal and very little iron. Japan had only a slight advantage over Italy; her coal was sufficient, but even with the mines of Manchukuo her supply of iron ore was insufficient. So she had to import iron, steel, and machinery. Many other countries were also poorly supplied with raw materials, for instance, the Scandinavian states. But these northern nations, especially Sweden, managed to achieve relatively high standards for their people by aiding the small landowner, by establishing controlled capitalism, by expanding the coöperative movement, and by introducing an extensive social legislative and insurance program.

On the other hand, a survey of the resources of the so-called satiated powers only serves to emphasize the inequalities which existed in national wealth. The United States was, by far, the richest of all. She possessed an adequate supply of nearly all the primary raw materials, and produced more than enough to feed her people. At the same time, she was not entirely self-sufficient, for she had to import rubber, tin, nickel, wool, silk, manganese, and other minor raw materials.

The Soviet Union, as far as raw materials were concerned, was also a satiated state. She had a surplus of oil, manganese, and chromium, and had more than an adequate food supply.

Great Britain herself was very poor in resources, with a reserve supply of coal only. But her empire as a whole was even richer than the United States, possessing practically all the essential raw materials and foodstuffs. Largely because of her reliance on her empire for these things, Great Britain realized that her existence depended upon her ability to rule the seas.

France's supply of raw materials, even taking her colonies into account, was far from adequate. Of the primary raw materials she had a surplus of iron only. Her colonies provided other items, but she still had insufficient coal, nickel, oil, copper, and other essentials. On the other hand, France produced her own food, and the French peasant and his land, even after the first World War, continued to be the foundation of French economy.

This brief analysis shows clearly that inequalities between nations existed—in land, population, and resources,—thus accentuating the post-World War problem of the unsatiated states. But in spite of certain justifiable demands of the "have not" powers for territorial changes, it was impossible, under the system of intense nationalism which developed after the War of 1914–1918, to expect a redistribution of lands with a view to giving the dissatisfied states a greater share of the essential raw materials. Such a solution of the problem might have been feasible if there had existed some form of international organization capable of working out and enforcing the territorial changes. But without such an agency, the problem of the unsatiated states was not merely economic, it was political and military. Any attempt to hand over raw materials to the "have not" powers, asserted certain elements in the "have" nations, would only aid the "have nots" in their aim, through power politics, to attain world supremacy.

Granted that redistribution of raw materials was not feasible, the crux of the whole problem of the unsatiated states seemed at that time to be a question of trade and markets and the factors which limited the purchasing power of the con-

sumer nations. Before the outbreak of the present war, it was
often suggested that the "haves" open up the markets of the
world to the unsatiated states and enable them to make
money enough to purchase raw materials and foodstuffs. But
this was not an easy thing to do. To buy and sell under the
democratic capitalistic system of international trade, a nation
had to have a favorable trade balance, or a gold reserve sufficient to balance its account. Inasmuch as most nations had
only a limited amount of gold, trade could not be carried on
for long on such a basis. In short, commerce between nations
must be an exchange of goods or of services.

After the first World War, a situation developed wherein
all nations, satiated and unsatiated, wanted to sell but not to
buy. The unsatiated states, according to Hitler, had to export
or face economic extinction, while the satiated nations, even
though they had a major part of the world's gold supply and
possessed, directly or indirectly, the essential raw materials
and foodstuffs, insisted that the improvement of their standard of living was dependent upon their ability to acquire new
and retain old markets. Facing such intense postwar problems as unemployment, debts, and dwindling trade, they too
were bent upon the restoration of economic progress through
the expansion of foreign trade.

The struggle for markets was not peculiar to the post-World
War period; it had been going on since ancient times. But it
reached a definite crisis in its evolution prior to the outbreak
of the present European conflict.

This crisis was the world-wide depression of 1929, which
brought about the collapse of the international banking sys-

tem, further disrupted trade, shattered the economic machinery of the world, and precipitated a bitter economic struggle among all nations, satiated and unsatiated, which finally resulted in the present war.

The terrible economic breakdown was not only a result of the terrific cost of the World War and the armament race thereafter; it was also an inevitable by-product of the unjust features of the peace treaties, and the mistakes made by the victorious Allies after the conflict. At the peace conference the democratic powers worked out territorial, commercial, and financial adjustments designed to destroy Germany's military and economic power. In order to do this, they deprived her of valuable raw materials, land, agricultural products, and her merchant marine, colonies, and foreign investments; they virtually destroyed her foreign trade by various restrictions; and they forced her to go through bankruptcy as a result of the imposition of heavy financial reparations. Thus they demoted Germany, which, before the war, was rapidly becoming one of the satiated states, to the ranks of the "have not" group.

While the Allies—France, Britain, and the United States— were making Germany an unsatiated state, they at the same time refused to promote their unsatiated partners in the war, Italy and Japan. Italy was given certain territorial rewards, but she did not receive the share of the German holdings that she said the Allies had promised her for entering the war on their side. Japan also was not satisfied with what she got out of the struggle. Taking advantage of the preoccupation of the Allies during the war, she had presented to China (in 1915) an ultimatum known as the Twenty-One Demands, tantamount to the establishment of a Japanese protectorate over China. Unable to obtain the acceptance of all demands by her coveted neighbor, Japan arranged agreements with China, Russia, Great Britain, France, and Italy whereby she secured virtually a free hand in northern China. This award, however, was practically nullified when Japan, at the Washington Conference (1921), returned the German holding of Shantung to China and entered into pacts with Great Britain, France, the United States, and other interested powers, guaranteeing the independence of China and the maintenance of the status quo in the Far East.

Thus the Allies, while they greatly increased their holdings as a result of the war, at the same time greatly endangered their positions by making three nations—Germany, Italy, and Japan—thoroughly dissatisfied. This situation, together with the menace of post-War Communism, should have caused them to recognize the need of some effective organization to maintain the newly established status quo.

But the United States refused to participate in the one organization capable of maintaining or of improving the new order, the League of Nations. Instead, we washed our hands of European affairs and adopted a policy of splendid isolation.

France, alone, became the staunch defender of the status quo. Afraid of a German war of revenge, and without the support of her former Allies, Great Britain and this country, she proceeded to establish her hegemony in Europe by maintaining a powerful army, by arranging alliances with Germany's enemies in Europe, and by using the League of Nations to carry out part of her program. At the same time she hastened Germany's disintegration by insisting that Germany and her former Allies fulfill all the terms of the peace treaties, including reparations payments.

This policy only served to bring about chaotic conditions in central Europe. The situation finally became so bad that the Allies, fearing a proletarian revolution in this part of Europe, intervened. Money was lent to the prostrate states, Germany, Austria, and Hungary; Franco-German relations were improved as a result of the Locarno Conference, in which Germany recognized the post-War frontier on the west as permanent; Germany was aided by the Dawes reparations settlement (1924); and the cause of collective security, many thought, was advanced when Germany was admitted to the League of Nations (1926).

For a few years it looked as though the unsatiated states were going to experience a real era of economic recovery. German trade expanded; Italian finances improved; and Japan managed to increase her export of goods, especially to the United States, China, and India. But this economic recovery came to an end about 1929–1930, when the satiated States (France, Britain, and the United States), in their attempt to recover from the effects of the World War, precipitated the World Depression.

It is a pretty well established fact that the war of 1914–1918 laid bare the weaknesses of industrial and finance capitalism— weaknesses only too prevalent in decadent pre-War England. Practically every nation, once the struggle was over, faced ugly economic and social problems. Millions of men and women were unemployed, industry and trade threatened to collapse, and monetary systems were completely disorganized. These troubles caused many reformers to favor drastic changes in the capitalistic system. Some advocated its abolition; others maintained that it should be absorbed by the totalitarian state; while many asserted that at least it should be controlled by the government.

The ruling groups in the important satiated states, Great Britain, France, and the United States, however, utterly opposed the introduction of these ideas in their political and social systems. In their opinion, private industry, personal initiative, and unrestricted production and economic expansion would alone bring about recovery. In short, free business enterprise in each state was to work out its own economic salvation.

Private business in these three countries did make a desperate attempt to lead the people around the proverbial Hooverian corner to prosperity. In France, big business (the Bank of France) attempted to bring about recovery by forcing the Germans to pay for the war, by attempting to obtain indirectly, if not directly, the left bank of the Rhine, and by exploiting the resources and dominating the markets of central and southeastern Europe. But the Germans failed to pay and the attempt to dominate central and southeastern Europe proved a bad investment. Facing a huge debt and a rapidly declining franc as a result of these policies, Premier Poincaré, representative of French finance capitalism, tried to stabilize the franc and revive business (1926). To reach these ends, he placed a large part of the burden of taxes on the thrifty middle classes and wage earners by devaluating the franc, thus depriving the bourgeoisie and also the peasant bondholders of four-fifths of their capital. At the same time he cheapened the franc by this manipulation of the currency, and enabled the industrialists for a short time to undersell their competitors in foreign markets.

For a few years France seemed to be on the road to recovery. She was able to feed and employ her numerically stationary population, to increase her gold reserve, and to expand her production. But as a result of her determination to build a powerful Maginot Line, and to support her post-War allies by financial loans, France dissipated her resources. Continued currency inflation, hastened by these expenditures, and a decline of foreign trade, finally prepared the way for French inclusion in the World Depression.

During the post-War period, Great Britain also had trouble in her attempt to attain economic prosperity. For a short while after the War, she enjoyed a period of moderate recovery. But in 1921 the boom had collapsed because of insufficient foreign markets and the serious competition of the United States, Germany, and France. England now faced a serious breakdown of her economic system, owing to high taxes, debts, increasing unemployment, and dwindling trade. Bravely she accepted Prime Minister Baldwin's conservative policy of "do nothing and everything will come out all right in the end." Half-heartedly she permitted Laborite MacDonald to arrange a trade agreement with Soviet Russia, and to encourage disarmament, hoping that these policies would somehow bring about a reversal of British fortunes. But prosperity simply refused to turn the corner. Then, in the early 'thirties, Great

Britain, like the other industrial nations, felt the effects of a sharp decline in economic activity—the great depression. This time she faced complete economic ruin.

The terrible crisis even affected the United States, youngest and strongest of the great capitalistic powers. After the war, she engaged in a rugged attempt to return to normalcy. But instead she experienced a few years of artificial prosperity which came to an end with the market collapse of 1929. At that time came the traditional sign of approaching depression, namely, a tightening of trade and investment rates. Credit was restricted; business activity slowed to a standstill; widespread unemployment resulted; and many businessmen, farmers, and bankers experienced economic extinction.

Facing a real crisis, the three great satiated states now engaged in a desperate struggle to save their capitalistic hides. In 1930, three years before Adolf Hitler came to power, our Congress passed the unhappy Hawley-Smoot Tariff Bill, designed to protect markets for Americans and to stimulate business thereby. Thus we announced to the other depressed unsatiated and satiated nations of the world that we were perfectly willing to sell goods to them, but we would not permit them to sell us goods and raw materials that competed with American products, even though the rest of the world owed us billions of dollars which they could only pay by selling to us. Meanwhile, to stimulate industry, President Roosevelt in 1934 decided to manipulate the currency, cutting the dollar to fifty-nine cents. On February 1, 1934, he prepared the way for the creation of a huge pile of gold by sanctioning its purchase at the high price of thirty-five dollars an ounce.

While the United States was trying to revive industry, to expand markets, and to prepare for the proverbial rainy day, Great Britain inaugurated a system of retrenchment designed to lower the tax burden on industry and at the same time to bring about a general business recovery. Like the United States, she decided to undersell the other fellows by going off the gold standard and thus cheapening the English pound. At the same time she endeavored to help industry by refusing to pay interest on the debt she owed this country and by establishing a British Imperial preference system at Ottawa—a kind of *Zollverein*.

Nor did France stay out of this economic war for markets. At a time when social democracy was bleeding to death in Germany, France created a web of preferential arrangements with the various parts of her empire—Tunisia, New Caledonia, French India, French Indo-China, Madagascar, French Guiana, and Algeria. She also decided to pay no interest on the debt due the United States, and determined to protect her industries by "elaborating a favorite trade-strangling device—the quota system of limiting imports." She also manipulated her currency with the view of stimulating her export trade. In short, the satiated States (in their attempts to avoid an internal economic crash) resorted to the economic nationalism of the 19th century, including many features of national capitalism (mecantilism) of early modern days.

The unsatiated lands did not have a sufficient amount of raw materials and gold to participate in this old-fashioned game of "trade war." And thus was driven home to them the fact that they were indeed "have not" powers. But why enter a game with those who possess money and raw materials and thus can play for huge stakes? Would it not be better for the unsatiated states to try the difficult but honest way, and, like other small "have not" nations (Sweden, for example), make the best use of what they had? "Nein! Nein!" was Hitler's reply to this suggestion; "Germany must demolish the unjust Treaty of Versailles; Germany must have living room; Germany must export—or die!" "Go ahead and die," was the unwritten reply of bitter anti-Nazis to this dramatic plea.

Meanwhile, the unsatiated gamblers organized their own game, which they called the "War against Communism and for Satiation." Benito Mussolini, in participating in this contest, stopped worrying about balancing the budget and started concentrating upon a policy of imperial expansion. "Italy has need of expansion," he cried, "and expand she will, despite the selfish embargo placed on her ambitions by the older colonizing powers of the Peace Conference." Thereupon he conquered Ethiopia (1936). Shortly after this imperialistic venture, Mussolini, in order to prove that the game was essentially one directed against Communism, helped Franco chase the so-called "Reds" out of Spain.

Developments forced Japan to participate in this crusade against Communism. Before joining this group, however, Japan had tried to play the other fellow's game. Bent upon becoming a great industrial power, she had, during the post-War period of depression, permitted the yen to depreciate some 68 per cent, "thus giving her textile manufacturers a bounty superior to that which England's depreciation had presented to the textile exporters of Lancashire." When angry

Britishers said unkind things about the Japanese unfair trade tactics, Tokyo simply replied, "But the Honorable John Bull started it."

Following the depression in the early 'thirties, Japan encountered sharply declining markets in the United States, India, and China (the result of a boycott). With dwindling gold reserves, she faced economic ruin and soon decided that she could best play the Italo-German game. Accordingly, she inaugurated her policy of imperialist expansion in China, announced a Monroe Doctrine of the Far East, and proclaimed her hostility to Russian Communism.

Germany, however, assumed the leading role in this contest to extinguish radicalism and to attain satiation. With the coming of the World Depression she discovered that she was in no position to play the old-fashioned game. German production in the spring of 1928 was 40 per cent above the low of 1926. But toward the end of the year a business recession had begun. In 1929 the extended conferences over the matter of reparations (the proposed Young Plan) caused a great deal of fear and unrest in the world's financial markets. Huge amounts of money (credits) were withdrawn from Germany, exerting severe pressure on German foreign exchange. With the stock-market crash in this country, American and British loans (more than 3 billion dollars in all) to Germany ceased, and money, the lifeblood of German production, was lost. At that time she possessed excellent technical equipment and industrial techniques, thanks to British and American financial aid, but she simply could not operate her industrial machine without raw materials and money.

Germany now entered another period of depression. Industry dropped 40 per cent; prices fell greatly in all fields of economic endeavor; and unemployment reached the alarming figure of 5,670,000. Thus the attempt of Republican Germany to attain satiation with the help of the capitalistic democracies had proved a failure. By the early 'thirties these nations, confronted by similar problems, were in no position to help any other country. As stated before, each government decided that the best way to solve the World Depression was to put its own house in order.

To accomplish this task, the Germans decided to undergo a thorough housecleaning. The Republic was abolished, and Hitler, head of the Nazi party, was called to the chancellorship. With the support of certain business interests he proceeded to exterminate Communism in Germany, expel all non-German elements, and regiment labor and, later, capital. His objective, as one contemporary writer viewed it, was to build "a strong, self-contained Germany, free from the sapping of international Jews and moneylenders, raising all the capital it needs at home, paying no tribute, withdrawing from the world of international business, being entirely self-sufficient and consuming all its products ... except exports necessary for the purchase of foodstuffs."

At first the conservative elements in the satiated states welcomed the rise of Hitler, believing that, like Mussolini, he would check the advance of Communism. In a short time, however, Hitler demonstrated that he intended not only to eliminate radicalism, but also to attain satiation for Germany through the restoration of German military power, arming not only in a military way, but economically and socially as well. For to Der Führer war had to be totalitarian, utilizing all the fighting powers of the nation.

At first the National Socialist government, possessing some romantic notions about autarchy, or a closed economy, adopted a policy of retrenchment and isolation. Withdrawing from the disarmament congress and the League of Nations, Nazi Germany immediately opened her campaign against the Versailles treaty, and announced that she was going to solve her own economic problems. But she could not withdraw from the field of industrial trade. She needed coal, iron, and ore for production purposes, and therefore had to sell in order to obtain these and other materials.

But where and how were the Germans to obtain markets for their goods? When the depression started, the Germans, who had already experienced a period of complete inflation, were afraid to revive industry by again tinkering with the currency. Consequently, with most of the other nations depreciating their money in order to export goods, Germany's mark stuck out like a sore thumb, becoming so expensive that foreign traders could not afford to purchase it. To make matters worse, the cessation of foreign lending by Great Britain and the United States, especially, had left Germany without enough foreign exchange "either to service foreign debts or to finance German imports."

Fortunately for the Nazis, they were able to place the German financial problem in the hands of Doctor Hjalmar Horace Greeley Schacht, the opportunistic Dano-German who had once headed the Reichsbank. As a liberal, Schacht believed that autarchy was suicide for a nation that lacked raw materials. But because his French, English, and American friends were not able to see the foolishness of trying to collect reparations from a country that was not able to export on even terms with other states, Dr. Schacht decided to carry out the Nazi program of the closed economy. At the same time, he asserted that this was but a temporary solution of the problem, which he hoped would help Germany to survive the World Depression. Then Germany would return to the old ways of carrying on international trade. Accordingly, he proceeded to repudiate not only the war debts, but also to stop the transfer, redemption, and interest payments on freely contracted loans of German public and private corporations. When these bonds fell, even beyond depression values, Schacht bought them up and thus extinguished a good part of the German debt. At the same time, Germans who held foreign stocks were forced to sell these securities to the German Reichsbank at a price much less than they could have obtained if they had sold them on the New York or London exchange. Schacht later sold these equities at a nice profit, which he used for subsidizing German exports.

Meanwhile, Hitler developed his policy of a war economy. This program made it necessary for the Nazis to purchase abroad such important military materials as iron, copper, and oil. At the same time, exports had to be cut down in order to concentrate everything and everybody in the construction of a military machine.

Herr Schacht, still professing to believe that this war-economy business was a temporary development, introduced the system of bilateral barter, "with exports going more and more to those countries that were prepared to trade Germany the raw materials." Export subsidies as great as 30 per cent of the value of all German exports enabled Nazi businessmen to exchange their goods in the Balkans and in South America for oil, grain, tobacco, cotton, and coffee. Frequently, the Nazis demoralized world markets for their suppliers by re-selling these goods at knockdown prices in order to obtain needed foreign exchange. As a result of this policy, German exports to southeastern Europe and Hispanic America in-creased, while exports to western Europe, the United States, and Soviet Russia fell off.

While establishing the barter system, Dr. Schacht also ma-nipulated the mark in such a way "as to put all foreign assets in Germany under protective arrest." The purpose of these various kinds of marks—travel marks, credit-blocked marks, compensation marks, and *Aski* marks—was primarily to cre-ate a situation in which Germany "stood ready to sell a certain amount of goods to whoever owned the block credit." Thus "international trade under this plan was to be carried on by regimented nations exchanging goods, rather than by indi-viduals, who under the democratic system of international exchange were able to engage in trade without governmental interference and support." Accompanying this German sys-tem of barter was a very efficient program of propaganda, designed to bring Hispanic American states, especially, into the German economic orbit.

In 1938, Great Britain, France, and the United States de-cided that this system of barter was not a temporary measure to achieve trading advantages under a peace economy. Instead, they concluded that it was an adjunct to a war economy whereby Germany was to abolish the Versailles settlements, secure living room, markets, raw materials, and territories—by power politics and, if necessary, by war.

The satiated states also realized that Japanese expansion and Italian activities in the Mediterranean were not exactly crusades against Communism. Consequently, the conservatives in Great Britain and France, after the totalitarian states had obligingly obliterated the Popular Front government in Spain, decided to adopt protective measures. A close military alliance was concluded between the two powers, and Great Britain inaugurated a five-year armament program, as a counterchallenge to the well-prepared "have not" powers. Meanwhile, Chamberlain began his appeasement plan designed to delay, if not avoid, the seemingly inevitable conflict between the two groups.

Having extinguished radicalism in western Europe (Spain), the unsatiated states now proceeded to outline their programs of expansion under the following headings: abolition of the Versailles treaty, a place for Italy in the Mediterranean, and China for Japan.

Thereupon, President Roosevelt and others vaguely suggested that a meeting be held for the purpose of arranging settlements which would help the unsatiated powers in their attempts to satisfy their peacetime economic needs. It was even stated that certain tentative settlements might be arranged. But neither side paid much attention to these proposals. The unsatiated powers, especially Germany, took the position that the threat of force was the only language the "haves" could understand, while the English refused to be forced to make concessions.

Germany's demands for a return of pre-World War holdings, involving the cession of French and British possessions, were bitterly opposed by liberal as well as by conservative Englishmen and Frenchmen. "If we could return to Germany her pre-War resources and put her back to her magnificent pre-War position," wrote Norman Angell, "we know that that of itself would not give us peace, for when she had those resources and that position Europe drifted to war."

In rejecting the German requests for the return of her colonies, some English writers even turned their backs on Kipling, saying that the whole notion of empire was a fantasy, an illusion. "We do not possess the wealth of, say, Canada (or India, or Africa), and we cannot in consequence give it away any more than the London County Council could give away the inhabitants of parts of London."

The demand of the "have not" powers for self-sufficiency also seemed irrelevant. "If self-sufficiency—great resources within political control—is the means of solving economic difficulties, why is Great Britain, possessing the greatest empire the world has known, the most heavily taxed nation in the world, with grave economic problems? Why does the United States, the most self-sufficient nation in the world, have sixteen million unemployed, while little states like the Scandinavian, having no empire, may nevertheless possess as high a standard of living as any in the world and meet their economic troubles with no great difficulty?"

Self-sufficiency, these writers explained, was unnecessary because no industrial country has ever, in time of peace, found itself discriminated against in the matter of access to raw materials. Other things being equal, most owners of raw materials will sell to those people who have cash, credit, or products, regardless of country.

Most of these scribes, however, ignored the fundamental issue between the two groups, namely, control of markets and money. The real difficulty, perhaps, was not lack of raw materials or any denials of access thereto, or any need of bringing them within the borders of each nation (a physical impossibility in any case), but, rather, was the creation of so many barriers to effective international coöperation and international trade that raw materials could not be paid for. If these barriers could have been removed, or at least modified, the world might have emerged from the depression and the present war would have been avoided.

But as we look back at the situation, such a solution was not practical, unless there was some kind of international organization capable of enacting the reforms and of enforcing them. Without this organization, it was logical that the unsatiated nations would resort to power politics and to war.

An understanding, therefore, of the basic significance of the trade war of the past few years forces one to realize that this present war is not simply a struggle between the "haves" and the "have nots." In his desire to reach his objective, Hitler seems determined to permit the issue to become even more fundamental. For, as I see it, Hitler, the man who has absorbed capitalism, was perfectly willing to accept the support of Stalin, the man who has smashed capitalism, in order to bring about the downfall of the Western political and social system (he calls it "plutocracy") and thus insure the supremacy of the authoritarian state.

Meanwhile, in the United States of America today there exists an important part of the Maginot Line of capitalist-democratic defense, as well as one of the fundamental reasons for the whole struggle. Some thirty miles southeast of Louisville, Kentucky, in a corner of the Fort Knox army reservation, there is a powerful building. Its roof and inner walls are of steel and concrete so thickly piled together that no aerial bomb now known to the army ordnance service can pierce them. The building is protected by machine-gun pillboxes at the four corners. Two massive doors bar the entrance to the building—doors that swing open only after two guards have coördinated the individual locks on them, and since no one guard knows the combination for both doors, the two men must always be present. Every half hour an alarm registers at headquarters and a check-up of the doors is then made.

There is a sign on the building which reads, "United States Depository." But it might as well read, "Midas, Incorporated." For, as a result of our policy of purchasing gold at thirty-five dollars an ounce, we possessed in the spring of 1939 more than one-half the known world's gold reserve, almost five and one-half times what was needed to back our currency. More than one-third of this amount was in Fort Knox. While this was being augmented, "people in large areas of the world were starving for the wherewithal to buy foreign exchange and so finance international trade."

"This gold at Fort Knox has neither eyes nor ears; if you prick it, it does not bleed. But you don't need much imagination to picture it as possessing a peculiar blood pressure of its own. In spite of the steel and concrete, the Fort Knox gold was silently pushing to get out into the world and go to work." Lack of it in the "have not" countries had forced them to introduce stringent trade restrictions to protect currency—restrictions that involved carefully cutting down imports to balance exports, and fiercely pushing exports with the view of obtaining foreign exchange with which to buy raw materials in order to live—or to rearm.

But why was not this flow of gold reversed; say, by setting a less attractive price per ounce on gold? "Why was not the curse of Midas thrown off?" It is true that much of the gold flowed to this country because the world needed our manufactured goods, raw materials, and foodstuffs, and because capitalism elsewhere was nervous and considered the United States the safest place in which to put its money.

But why didn't the "have" powers export the excess of liquid capital in such a way as to stimulate production and trade, thus bringing about world recovery? In the past, England, Holland, Belgium, and other "have" states, used the profits that they accumulated to build railroads, warehouses, meat-packing plants, and factories in overseas countries, with the result that markets expanded everywhere. "But the twentieth century apparently does not learn from the nineteenth," and, in spite of its tremendous wealth, even the United States seemed powerless or unwilling to devise profitable ways of financing industrial trade expansion through the export of capital. Consequently, "a situation had developed (by 1939) where the 'have' nations were stymied, and the 'have not' nations became desperate." A showdown seemed inevitable. Thus the war is fundamentally a struggle between the "haves" and the "have nots," with two types of economy—finance capitalism and state capitalism—fighting to prevail.

It is generally hoped in this country that the so-called democratic capitalism of a large part of the world will survive the struggle and that Germany, the leader of the unsatiated group, will be defeated. But will that happen? And if it does, what next? Will the so-called satiated states be able to develop sufficient unity of action to establish and maintain a peaceful and prosperous democratic and capitalist world—if that is not a paradox? Will they not only introduce necessary internal reforms, but also finally become internationally minded, carry out the idealistic program inaugurated by Woodrow Wilson, and, by constructive and just legislation designed to eliminate the marked inequalities of today, justify their right to lead? Or will the modern democracies, like many of their shortsighted predecessors, relinquish their position in the vanguard of civilization? Like the ancient Greek and early modern Italian and Dutch city-states, will they fall as a result of their stubborn insistence on an anachronistic localism, their foolish reliance on compromise, and their false worship of Midas gold?

Perhaps that famous English politician and poet of the 14th century, Chaucer, pictures the ultimate result of the selfish struggle between the satiated and unsatiated powers in the tale of his Pardoner in the Canterbury cycle.

"The love of money is the root of evil" is the text which Chaucer takes from Timothy's epistle (chap. 6) and, to illustrate, he tells the story of the ancient revelers who go in search of Death, to slay him, for Death has taken away many of their friends. They meet an old man, who informs them that they will find Death under a certain tree upon a crooked way. But instead of Death they discover a hoard of golden coins, and speedily forget their former quest.

One of the three rascals is dispatched to the town to get bread and wine and a donkey upon which to carry the gold home, under cover of darkness. The remaining two plot to kill him when he returns so that the "split" will be only a two-way one. This they do with ease, and then sit down to refresh themselves before they move their treasure, each one probably contemplating the murder of the other so that no division will be necessary. But alas! the one who had gone into town had a similar idea, and Chaucer tells us that from an apothecary this one got poison "to kill the rats and the polecats which had been eating his chickens," which poison he put in the wine, so that when the two survivors emptied their glasses they forthwith died in great agony.

The three sought Death, and found him unexpectedly. They were "have nots"; then they were "haves"; then all they had gained was of no avail.

Will Western civilization find Death under an oak tree?

THE DEMAND FOR A
REDISTRIBUTION OF COLONIES:
POLITICAL AND ECONOMIC
ASPECTS

———

MELVIN M. KNIGHT
PROFESSOR OF ECONOMICS
IN THE UNIVERSITY OF CALIFORNIA

Lecture delivered October 17, 1939

THE DEMAND FOR A
REDISTRIBUTION OF COLONIES:
POLITICAL AND ECONOMIC
ASPECTS

To GET AT the meaning of "colonies" for this subject, and hence to realize what it is that could possibly be redistributed, some very common misconceptions must be cleared away: first, the careless assumption that every detached part of a so-called "colonial empire" is a colony; second, the confusion of sovereignty with property, or the notion that the mother country "owns" its colonies; and third, the supposition that resources imported from colonies are necessarily cheap.

Dr. Schacht, the German financial wizard, wrote in 1937 (*Foreign Affairs*) that the "British Empire" had "more than a quarter of the earth's surface at its disposal," this area supplying eighteen of the "estimated twenty-five varieties of essential raw materials." Since the comparison was with poor, disinherited Germany, a European state, it should have restricted itself to the territories really controlled by the European member of the "British Empire," or the United Kingdom. Independent associates like Canada and Australia should not be included; nor does the United Kingdom have "at its disposal" the produce of economically autonomous units like India, save on terms of negotiation and payment. Algeria is not a colony, but an economically assimilated territory, politically represented in the French parliament.

Since Italians have made so much officially inspired noise about Tunisia, a protectorate of France, we may stretch the meaning of "colony" to include all protectorates. German official clamor for the return of former colonies which are now mandates under the League of Nations may prompt us to consider all mandates as colonies. Class A mandates, being quite temporary trusteeships, should not be included, of course, but let us stretch the point.

The colonies, protectorates, and mandates of the United Kingdom cover 2.4 millions of square miles, which is a twenty-fourth of the earth's land surface, not a fourth. These areas have a combined population of 61.5 millions, or about a thirty-first of the world total, and an economic output which is a very tiny fraction of the whole. The colonies, protectorates, and mandates of all the nations add up to less than a fourth of the world's land surface, and to descending fractions of the population and output. The items are far from being what Dr. Schacht hinted at; but they are large.

In terms of surface, the largest shares are those of France, the United Kingdom, Italy (counting Ethiopia), Belgium, Portugal, The Netherlands, and the United States, in that order. Japan ranks fourth in colonial population, with 29 millions, but the area is relatively small, not counting any of China proper. Germany is the conspicuous "have not" among the great powers. As we shall see presently, colonies are particularly unimpressive as sources of industrial raw materials.

That the advantages of sovereignty and of property are quite different questions is of the utmost importance for this discussion. Since the Italians have made special mention of

Tunisia (Americans sometimes call the country Tunis, after its capital city), let us use it for an illustration. Theoretically, and to an appreciable degree in fact, Tunisia is still ruled by a native government with a Bey at its head. A protectorate treaty gives France the right to handle foreign and military affairs and to exercise a great deal of supervision over the government. This is mainly indirect rule, as distinguished from direct rule in a typical colony, where the "mother country" has full sovereignty and the laws are issued and administered by her own officials. France's sovereignty is further limited in Tunisia—much more so in Morocco—by treaty rights which other powers had before the protectorates were established, and by later treaties confirming those rights. In Tunisia, Italian rights are by far the most important of these.

France does not "own" the Tunisian land or the two million native Tunisians who occupy most of it. She merely has limited rights of sovereignty over it and them. Some ninety thousand French citizens and ninety thousand Italian citizens in Tunisia own a good deal of land, but the French state owns very little. I have been in Tunisia a number of times, and talked with many people of high and low degree. When the question arises of what would be changed if France should transfer her limited sovereignty to Italy, I let these people supply most of the answers.

First, more official jobs would be open to Italians, fewer to Frenchmen. Second, Frenchmen would not have exactly the same personal rights and security of property which both Frenchmen and Italians now have. Third, and far more important as far as I am concerned, neither would Tunisians.

I do not mean that the Italians would kick the Tunisians around, physically; but it is a sound bet that a great deal more land would be taken from natives for Italian colonists, and that Tunisians would have less chance to live as they like to, on the lands of their fathers. Fourth, Italy would have forts on both sides and in the middle of the bottleneck between the western and eastern halves of the Mediterranean. Fifth, Algeria and the routes southward to French Tropical Africa would not be so secure as they are now. Sixth, a considerable number of excellent soldiers would shift sides, should the appeasement fail to appease.

The seventh point is in some ways a broader statement of the third, concerning native rights. In Tunisia, as in much of the world, a "decolonization" or "countercolonization" process has been at work. Tunisians have increased their voice in their own affairs and have even recovered land from Europeans. The peace settlements after the Great War, with their emphasis upon native welfare in mandates, gave decolonization and access to colonial trade a stimulus which has not been entirely lost. Giving Tanganyika back to Germany would involve specific issues of this sort. For example, British administrators required the Territory to purchase and hand back to natives lands which had been taken for European colonization to the extent of disrupting native life. Authority of which native chiefs had been deprived was restored. France, Britain, and Belgium all made substantial concessions to their subject peoples after the war, partly as a moral obligation, in return for much-needed aid.

Many colonial trade doors were partly closed as depression

measures after 1929. Nor has this been the whole story of imperial closed-door maneuvers, as I have taken pains to point out in a little book on French Morocco. Still, the arrest and even reversal of the decolonization process is in danger of becoming much more pronounced and general.

Undoubtedly there is a great deal of self-interested humbug about the liberal humanitarianism of present colonial policies. Their tolerance may be ascribed largely to fatigue, satiety, and a conviction that most colonies are now economically burdensome. The fact remains that certain promising schemes for removing the burdensomeness are not applied because of fixed policies concerning native rights and welfare. Professor Bonn, one of the outstanding authorities on colonization in Imperial Germany and now an exile in England, has remarked that this refusal to rule arbitrarily in their own interests may be the greatest handicap of the British and French empires in defending themselves. Small wonder that Fascist discipline is proclaimed as not for export. One of the main hesitations of the imperial "haves" about transferring various degrees of colonial sovereignty to the more clamorous "have nots" rests upon the fear that such rights would be stiffened into something quite different. This may be stated very simply in these words: "If we gave you our limited sovereignty, you might proceed to remove the limits."

All I shall have time to say on the third question raised in the beginning, namely, whether resources imported by a country from its colonies are really cheap, may be covered incidentally by an eighth point concerning Tunisia. It is hard to see how France would suffer any serious national economic loss merely by giving up Tunisia. French imports from this protectorate are, in large part, competitive with France's own produce, and come in at high prices set within the domestic tariff wall. The disadvantages of paying far more than the goods could be purchased for outside the empire are too great to be offset by profits on a much smaller return trade. Besides this, there are budget deficits and investments which are none too certain of ever being recovered. The case of Morocco is even clearer. A like problem in the Philippines was in large part the reason for our attempt to launch them on their own keel. At least, we refused to give them up to anybody but themselves. The British were more inclined to take this solution with a knowing shrug, but it was fluently cursed in Indo-China and Java as desertion for mercenary motives.

It is quite easy to overlook important groups of debit items in connection with a national overseas venture. France charges herself most of the colonial military bill, on the ground that the forces are merely kept overseas instead of at home. Quotations of colonial securities on the Bourse are visible and impressive, but an endless string of failures, one at a time, is hardly noticed. Measures to encourage production in the colonies often raise prices to consumers at home without their being remotely aware of it. A radical Deputy once remarked to me: "Colonies are principally devices for milking French consumers to fatten special classes of Frenchmen."

Arguments that colonies do not pay as national investments have become very common in England. The position is basically sound, but the whole matter is not so easily covered. Besides questions of national prestige, of military strength, and of obligations already assumed toward weaker peoples, there is what Professor Robbins calls a negative advantage. In a nutshell, it is that the situation might be worse if investments already made were not protected, and if other nations were put in a position to close markets now open. The problem is a serious one in a world with conflicting forms of society, some of which seem to regard all concessions as leverages, and obligations as binding only when enforced in the literal sense.

The usual German retort to the statement that colonies are burdensome is: "Then why not give us some?" Hitler, who was originally anticolonial, has taken this up as a good debating position. In fact, colonies are not property, and the analogy with a business which does not pay is a very loose one. Even if it were strict, businesses which do not yield normal returns on capital and effort are not generally given away. Some can be reorganized, with more or less capital, and most of the others have a liquidation value. I am not aware that the owners of a string of factories have ever given one away, free and unconditionally, to a competitor.

Hitler spoke sarcastically in 1937 of foreign statesmen who asserted that colonies had no value and yet would not "hand back these worthless possessions to their legal owners." The reference was to the former German colonies. Legal ownership, used as an analogy with private property, is as weak as the one just mentioned. If the reference is to international law, it must be remembered that the German colonies were taken away by conquest, and the transfer regularized by a peace treaty. The notion that the acquisitions were "illegal" because

Germany was obliged to sign, having lost the war, is a baseless analogy with private transactions. A closer one would be to argue that the loser of a prize fight is robbed because his share of the gate is reduced by the force of his opponent.

Charges concerning "Germany's derelictions in the sphere of colonial civilization" by the Allied and Associated Powers were in large measure hypocritical, and I am not trying to whitewash them. The hunting down of the Hereros in Southwest Africa and of the Maji-Maji in East Africa occurred long before the Great War, and can be matched with other peoples' imperial behavior about the same time. Just before the outbreak of war in 1914, Great Britain entered into an understanding with Germany about dividing Portugal's colonies, should that country cease to rule them; so, if the Germans were derelict, the British were willing to become accessories. Neither that excuse nor the really valid one that the Allies wished to avoid the danger of scattered German bases appeared in the Versailles treaty. Mandates over these territories were made subject to burdensome obligations and restrictions which have much to do with the unprofitableness of most of the areas to the mandatory powers.

At the present time, Germany would not accept mandates over these territories, but demands full sovereignty, which is a quite different matter so far as making assets of them is concerned. There are property difficulties about such a transfer, for example, bonds for public improvements which might be expected to go the way of Austrian, Czech, and Polish foreign obligations. The question of military and submarine bases remains. Finally, German economic policy and currently proposed colonial innovations have disquieting features, some of which will be taken up presently.

Any attempt to pin colonial demands down to tangible meaning in the actual world must take cognizance of the fact that a war broke out in 1939, following a series of German military coups at the expense of her European neighbors. Surely no one imagines that all this could have been avoided merely by heeding casual German allusions to dubiously valuable lost colonies. Germany's trade with her colonies before the World War was barely over one-half of one per cent of the total. In all her African colonies, with fourteen million natives, there were twenty-four thousand Germans, troops included. There is little doubt that this lost empire became an issue as a token of equality in status with other nations. That was national sentiment, as was Hitler's passionate assertion in 1935 that Germans had as good a right as anybody to rule other races. The point now is, what are the demands in the present situation, and how should we interpret them in the light of it.

Hitler announced to his Reichstag on October 6, 1939, that the government and the people of Germany "no longer see cause or reason for any further revision of the [Versailles] treaty, apart from the demand for adequate colonial possessions, namely, in the first instance, for the return of the German colonies."

"This demand," he continued, "is based not only on Germany's historical claim to German colonies, but above all on her elementary right to a share of the world's resources of raw materials. This demand does not take the form of an ulti-

matum, nor is it a demand backed by force, but a demand
based on political justice and sane economic principles."

While the demand does not "take the form of an ultimatum" at present, what sort of "political justice and sane
economic principles," put into practice by others, are envisaged as the price of its not becoming an ultimatum? The first,
or token, concession in the new series is little more than
nominal in itself. "In the first instance," France and Britain
(mainly) are to return the former German colonies. Compared with the last of the previous series—the regularization
of all the grabs in central Europe—this dose is mild. It need
not even be taken the same day. Though the initial and token
delivery would naturally take place soon, as evidence of
French and British good faith, a slight delay may be allowed
if French and British statesmen need it in order to compose
their faces and prepare their fellow citizens. The important
step is the admission that Germany has a right and propor-
tionate share of colonial empires now ruled by other peoples.
If France and Britain underwrite this proposition, much
weaker powers, like Holland, Belgium, and Portugal, can
make little trouble about it, once the march of political justice
and sane economics gets under way.

Remember, the capitulation of France and Britain at this
point, in the hope of saving something, is mentioned here
only as a German proposal, and for the light it may shed upon
colonial demands which have not been built up much so far.
As Hitler has said over and over in the past, it was not yet
time, with so much to be done first. Repeatedly, he has done
little more than earmark the subject of colonial expansion for

future development. Anyway, Mussolini obligingly broke some imperial windows, having less to preoccupy him on his own borders.

One of the gravest risks in Germany's position is that France and Britain will see the handwriting and divide with Italy, instead of waiting to have their carcasses picked by Hitler and Mussolini together. The Soviets may have about all they can digest for the time being. Moreover, it is contiguous territory, which is much simpler to handle and defend than distant colonies. If Stalin is the unscrupulous realist as painted, he may not be much interested in strengthening the National brand of Socialism in central Europe.

What, then, are German "political justice and sane economic principles"? I am going to assume that Italian ideas are closely analogous, ignoring differences over details. For what sort of world game are the rules designed?

To begin with, it must be even more strictly a game of great powers than the present one. There is no talk of giving Switzerland, Sweden, or Denmark subject areas in proportion to their population or technical capacity. The two leading avowed objects of revision are economic self-sufficiency and room for cultural expansion for those self-consciously superb civilizations which realize that they are the light and hope of the world. No one of them could ever fully supply its economic needs within its own territories unless these included most of the earth's surface. Even the British Empire, the United States, and the Soviet Union are far from being economically self-sufficing.

As a few imperial powers should approach self-sufficiency,

however remotely, the remaining peoples would recede from it, becoming more and more dependent upon the lordly nations. I presume there is no point in speaking of little and big states as mere "neighbors" under such a dispensation. The only apparent hope that the great powers would not fight over their insufficiencies and cultural deserts seems to be that their number, and the even balance of military strength, would make fighting too dangerous. This sort of thing has been tried many times, only to go into grand smashups through lack of machinery for peaceful readjustments in a changing world.

If we appraise the present colonial areas as booty of the self-assertive and technically superior nations, we must make allowances for possible development, besides considering resources as now exploited. Thus Professor Bonn concedes the extreme possibility that Germany might get 15 per cent of her necessary imports of raw materials from her former colonies. We cannot go into the many estimates, or more or less expert guesses, here. The main reservation about such possibilities of increase is that a large fraction of them would be exploited now if there were not other and cheaper sources of the same materials. Therefore the presumption that they are uneconomical would have to be rebutted in each case.

Dr. Schacht's and Herr Hitler's retort to this is that Germany cannot buy raw materials in the world market "because she does not possess the means of paying for them in foreign currencies..." (Schacht). This inability, Dr. Schacht says, occurs because foreigners do not buy enough German wares. Herr Hitler says it is because "they" (not precisely identified) have "fleeced" Germany for years. One might suggest at least one other factor. Germany has been pouring her natural and human resources for years into military equipment and skill which were not even offered for sale. Not only was this an alternative use of available effort and materials; the strain also tended to force prices up in Germany and make exports difficult. Moreover, clever resorts to barter between countries not only took the place of freer market exchanges in the past, but also helped to dry up such exchanges or drive them elsewhere.

Recall the earlier point that produce from one's colonies is not free and may not even be cheap. The British comment on Dr. Schacht's position that Germany must have resources within her currency area is that they would have to be produced, transported, and paid for just the same. Great Britain buys nickel from Canada at the competitive prices which Canadian producers can get for it, and the dollar exchange which she must create in order to pay is foreign exchange.

Germans have proposed the same procedure with colonies that they have used with independent countries: buy dear in currency which can be spent only in Germany, and thus get most of the loss back by selling dear. By different methods which also result in high costs of living and expensive control, France has achieved much the same condition of mutually high prices in her empire, and has very nearly collapsed financially. The economizing of natural and human resources, in order to get the most out of each dose, is a field in which it is easier to point out that perpetual-motion schemes have not worked than to explain why they will not.

Most of the trade jam and the agitation for colonial revision have arisen since 1929. If we consider the depression years following, the fact which sticks out like a sore thumb is not that raw materials were scarce, but that it was difficult to pay for them with exports and impossible to get rid of them at remunerative prices.

At the Leipzig Fair in 1936, Herr Goebbels named six materials as basic to modern industrialism: coal, iron, oil, cotton, rubber, and copper. Of these, rubber is mainly colonial (roughly, 96 per cent); but there are artificial methods of producing it, at costs which are still high. The time may well be approaching when natural rubber will go the way of natural indigo. Copper is over 20 per cent colonial. The other four items range downward from petroleum—of which less than 4 per cent comes from colonies, protectorates, and mandates—to coal, the colonial sources of which are a tiny fraction of 1 per cent of the world total.

If we go into the vegetal oils, only palm and copra are mainly colonial, and there are substitutes, particularly satisfactory ones for copra. Colonies, in the broad sense we have adopted, are negligible as furnishers of textiles. A little over half the tin and phosphates, and a little under half the graphite, are of colonial origin. Of the really basic foodstuffs, only cane sugar is over a quarter colonial, and beet sugar is over three-quarters noncolonial. The League of Nations Committee on Raw Materials sifted out thirty-nine items as of major importance. Two of these (rubber and palm oil) were listed as almost exclusively colonial, four (cocoa, copra, tin, and phosphates) as mainly colonial, and six (tea, graphite, cane sugar, bananas, peanuts, and copper) as colonial to a consider-

able extent. Production of most of them could be increased,
the question being whether this would be the most economi-
cal way for humanity to spend its limited energies.

German colonies would take German goods in exchange
for their own produce on some terms. They would even favor
German goods, where most of the subject areas now discrimi-
nate against them in one way or another. Whether the terms
of trade would be better than those which Dr. Schacht says
Germany cannot now meet, depends upon the way the subject
areas are to be organized and administered. I doubt if Germany could bear the economic burden of running North
Africa alone the way the French do it, and I am very sure she
would not.

Before the Great War, German colonial methods were not
strikingly different from those of more experienced nations.
It is sometimes said that they were ahead of the Portuguese
but had not caught up with the British. The French criticized
the English, and the English the Germans, for a certain stiff-
ness. Like other German enterprise, colonization came late
and was thought by its competitors to be in too big a hurry to
catch up. Great Britain had acquired a certain wisdom, which
both France and Germany lacked, about not overdriving production or development. British students of colonization now
charge that the Germans, far from having learned from their
error, have incorporated more of it in the schemes devised
during the period of colonial inactivity.

From the British point of view, the Germans pressed European settlement much too hard in the few areas where they
seriously tried it, and were incautious, rather than inhumane,

about the effects upon native life. The German view, which I have never understood very well from their literature, was presented to me at great length by German scholars in 1935 and 1938, with the great advantage that the men, unlike the books, answered questions. Current Italian ideas have a good deal in common with current German ones. Both stress the integrity of the European cultures, and plan new safeguards; but really to believe the genetic dogmas about race, or to think that native policy can be manipulated from a dial, is too much for the Italian sense of humor.

Both Germans and Italians take the view that a great deal of European settlement in the tropics is feasible, given totalitarian discipline. Their scheme is to send practically mobilized groups to clear the healthier highlands and concentrate all natives in lowland cantons. Thus the native is to get a certain "welfare" in his own region, protected from the greed of white planter and merchant. It is hoped that a policy of separation, rather than of mixture with either equality or inequality, will avoid the corrosive influences which, say the enthusiasts, have wrecked such ventures in the past. One man told me he had visited German religious settlements in fully tropical Brazil, at no great altitude, and found them healthy, prolific, and prosperous after generations. If religion can preserve the necessary separation, said he, so can National Socialism. Such colonization would involve a paternalism of government which we can scarcely imagine, much less view with sympathy. Probably native troops, as well as native labor, would be inconsistent with the plan, which could never be carried out with free settlers.

Separateness of cultures is only one feature of this scheme, and has been tried. We are told that much of the amazing development of Palestine since the Great War was carried out with expensive Jewish labor rather than to prejudice the result. There again, however, we have a religious group, not a totalitarian government. Besides, Palestine is not tropical.

If much of the world is to be Nazified or Fascized in the sense of trying to keep "superior" and "inferior" peoples apart permanently, it will certainly be a very different world from that which modern times have imagined they were creating. While it is not part of my assignment, I merely call attention to the fact that the separation into "superior" and "inferior" peoples on the basis of force has actually struck down free nations in Europe first, and there is no telling where the process will stop. It has its supporting dogmas, too, ready made for application to black Africans. We read that the old Slavic frontier received all the civilization of which it was capable from central Europe, ran amuck, and had to be taken in charge again. How things have changed since a year or two ago, when the same people called the same occupants of Poland "a great and flourishing nation," and it was particularly the Slavs east of it who had been insufficiently civilized!

Possibly colonizable areas like upland Ethiopia may serve as safety valves for unemployment in Europe. The quarter of a million mobilized Italian workmen in that area now would presumably be jobless at home, and very likely causing more embarrassment than they do where they are. Many more of these work battalions are contemplated, and there is a scheme to convert these indented servants of the Italian state gradually and cheaply into proprietors with strictly white families. If it costs somewhat more than a dole, and even if it never pays the home country any net returns, it at least solves some current problems. Governments still have the depression psychology of spending, and do not seem to mind running into debt. If they cannot pay certain of their own citizens, all they have to do is to duck in one way or another, passing gradually and almost unobserved from one form of society into another. I suggest that the advocates of peaceful readjustment have not given this method the attention it deserves.

The clamor for colonial revision does not necessarily mean that any feasible readjustment would do any good at all. It is mostly a cry of pain, from hunger, fear, and uncertainty. For more than four centuries now, Europeanism has expanded pretty steadily in a world of limited size. Speculation on the bull side was generally good if the speculators could hold on long enough, while population, settled area, and the intensifying of production increased. Political and economic organization, social outlook, and the pattern of life otherwise, were made over to fit these conditions. Now they are in large part gone, and what was to be eternal is blowing around us in clouds of dust. Western civilization is milling about like a hive of bees with the queen gone. Some people would carry the analogy so far as to say that the workers are trying to lay eggs.

Western Europe is in the worst position. She has equipped and populated herself to supply the world with capital goods, manufactures, carrying services, and ideas, and to live in considerably better than average style, largely on what these exports would bring back in exchange. Now the rest of the world does not pay so well for so much of what Europe is set up to provide. Perhaps it would be possible for that continent to reorganize itself, and thus to take care of its dense population without the accustomed tribute from outside.

But we are creatures of habit and tradition. If expansion was the way out of little maladjustments in the past, men assume that it must be the way out of the end of an age in the present; this in spite of the fact that nearly all the wide and suitable areas for European settlement are occupied, that the cream of the great expansionist movement is otherwise practically skimmed, that most of the civilized populations are rapidly becoming stabilized, and that non-Europeans the world around have factored what we had to offer and set up for themselves, immune from conquest and exploitation by handfuls of white adventurers with guns in their hands. Neither to have nor to hold distant subjects is any longer cheap.

Italy is a peculiarly sad part of Europe's sad case. Her great contribution to expansion has been Italians by the tens of thousands, who made a high birthrate possible by their constant departure, sent remittances back home, and either took whole families out eventually or came back themselves to live up in Italy what they had earned elsewhere. The end of mass emigration was one of the main factors which gave the country economic claustrophobia and blew the old order higher than a kite. Italy's population density is over 350 per square mile, or roughly ten times ours, but we have immense natural resources while hers are exceptionally poor. What we may call her "economic density" is one of the highest in the world.

Germany also lost millions of her nationals to foreign lands, where they became separated from her citizenship and largely from her language and culture. Then a vast development of industry and trade practically stopped the exodus, making it possible for the increase to live comfortably at home. It is needless to recount here how Germany was worn down by the war and plucked by the peace. There was some improvement from about 1924 to 1929, but it is doubtful if the German standard of eating has ever caught up to that of 1914. Foreign investments were swept away by the war and the peace, and trade had to be built all over in a changed world. For one thing, Russia, a sort of "colonial" market for pre-War Germany, industrialized and cut herself off. A densely populated and highly industrialized country like Germany, equipped to work for and live from the wide world, is practically strangled in the European situation as it has obtained since 1929. The congestion of manufactures and population relative to markets and raw materials is not much relieved by the territorial seizures of the past thirteen months.

Japan's feeling that she must grab in order to be sure of trading is founded on home conditions similar enough to those described above not to require discussion here. China's gradual withdrawal from European economic domination has been one of the agonies of Europe. That withdrawal seems permanent, however the present "incident" may terminate.

The Great War probably helped to time the European transition from expansion to holding and eventual contraction. It may well have concentrated and increased the pains. For one, I cannot see that it did much more. Neither can I believe that the North Atlantic world is going to be a boy again after any one dose of medicine. The British imperial preference scheme of seven years ago was only the straw which broke the back of existing colonialism, but some straw was bound to be one too many. Whenever political sovereignty should be used generally to throttle the economic relations of others with vast imperial systems, the issue of who ruled was certain to be roused from fitful sleep.

I have tried to be modest with my subject, and to remember that colonization is only one part of a vast problem of rule and its relation to trade. Independent nations also have near-monopolies of materials, if they choose to assert them by political authority. This they had better be prepared to back by force. More damage was done to Europe by fences around the American market than by all the colonial restrictions combined. With the general "debtors' revolt" following the World War, and the collapse of the gold standard, the old tissue of more or less self-regulating world trade was rent to pieces. One may well wonder if anything could restore Humpty Dumpty to his wall.

A mass of ominous facts suggests that the end of the age in which we were born has already occurred. It is all too easy to think in terms of a system which is hardly even a façade any more, when we should be trying to separate the pure rubbish from the building materials which can still be fitted into a world capable of supporting a good life for two billion people. It is easy to say in such a transition period as ours that proposed new rules are "not cricket," and also to retort that we are not playing cricket any more or caring anything about it.

But no group has all the constructive proposals or all the rubbish and illusions which might well be discarded. For example, behind the new German gospel of civilization is the haunting remembrance that the Germans were once the great European colonizers. I refer to the Slavic frontier of medieval times. The external expansion of Europe since Columbus has buried that, and cannot be unlived. The special German hatred of England needs to be psychoanalyzed and purged. In the end, the completely decolonized free nations of British culture have turned out to be the only certainly valuable remains from what was once imperial rule. There is nothing that can be done about that, for it is a genetic product of history, not merely stamped on the surface. If domination is no longer any good, this is a fact to be faced, ruefully perhaps, but without defense mechanisms. But the totalitarians do not believe that such conquests are ended forever, and no abstract reasoning from bygone conditions can settle the question.

MANDATES VERSUS
THE IMPERIALISTIC SOLUTION

———

HERBERT INGRAM PRIESTLEY
PROFESSOR OF MEXICAN HISTORY
IN THE UNIVERSITY OF CALIFORNIA

Lecture delivered October 24, 1939

MANDATES VERSUS
THE IMPERIALISTIC SOLUTION

THE PHRASING of this topic suggests that one or other of the alternatives presented by it can be used with world-wide validity to control the backward raw-products parts of the world in such way as to restore and maintain that peace which has been destroyed through the pressure of international economic tensions. Either by some modification of imperialism or by some adaptation of the mandate system, the lack of certain basic raw products might be removed from the present causes of general disequilibrium and war. A long step might be taken toward resumption of the almost lost ideals of life, liberty, and the pursuit of happiness.

Although imperialism as a method of approach to economic solutions has had centuries of trial, it has not only thus far failed to create a livable world, but has grown with increasing acerbity to be the conditioning element in the present political and economic demoralization. The practice of the European expansive states has been, ever since the great adventure of Columbus, to seize for motives of "pride, prestige, and pugnacity" parts of the extra-European world, for the sake of advantages economic or political, usually for the control of markets and investments by manufacturing, exporting, and financial classes. Such seizures have often happened through some form of international agreement, as in the operation of the Berlin Conference (1884) in the partition of Africa; and again sometimes by joint pressure against an impotent victim, as in the establishment of spheres of influence in China, par-

ticularly after 1898. Usually perpetrated with vestiges of bad
conscience, they have been rationalized as spreading the blessings of Christianity, of antislavery, of democracy, or of advancement of conquered peoples in the usages of technical
civilization. In most recent episodes this excuse has not been
emphasized, the reasons alleged being those of necessity in
the face of the unjust advantages already possessed by some
competing aggressor state. Portugal, Spain, Holland, France,
and England have followed an almost uniform system of overseas conquest and domination since the 16th century; Germany and Italy, since the 1870's; the United States and Japan
entered the lists, with some modification by each, about 1898.
Russia sought to dominate the Pacific in the 18th century, and
spread her influence over non-Russian territories of Asia during the 19th.

The Great War of 1914–1918 was very largely developed out
of mutual tensions engendered in the seizures of North Africa
and the Near East. There were also trade discriminations and
policies of "encirclement" in which the Germans felt ham-
pered by British competition. At the conclusion of hostilities
a system was coördinated from various suggestions for the
purposes of substituting for the balance of power a voluntary
system of collective security for all the nations, and of providing at the same time a means of redistribution and proper control for the previous German and Turkish colonies, known
since as the mandate system. This dismemberment of the defeated empires was not conceived entirely as a solution of the
problem of dependent areas, but also as a means of satisfying
the vengeance and cupidity of the victors, and had inherent

in it defects of design—restriction of the mandate idea to the areas indicated, and the purpose of restraining the recupera- tion of Germany. The readjustment of European boundaries on the basis of ethnic self-determination neglected or violated essential economic necessities. Nevertheless, the mandate sys- tem showed for a time great capacity for partial solution of the colonial problem. But based as it was upon many of the essential characteristics of the imperial system, it was inaugu- rated with modifications which made of it a mere auxiliary of imperialism, and as a consequence its operation failed to become a major success of the League system of which it was a component. Since the recent breakdown of the League as an agency of international control, especially since the idea of empire has but yesterday undergone great reorientation, we have in reality an orphaned institution, the mandates, together with an ideal of empire as a national mechanism geared to little other than maximum war efficiency, and a system of balance of power, operated by dictatorial pronouncements, collusion, and threats, as the essential background of any pros- pective reconstruction of a workable world society. From the debris of this double ruin we must weave a new fabric for our economies, and for our political intercourse.

The so-called National Socialist program, prosecuted since 1933, offers startling modifications of the imperialistic method. Its evolution was insidious, in that the quest for restoration of German rights, wrested away in 1919, contemplated recon- quest of territory within the confines of an alleged Germanic ethnic empire. Moreover, reaction against the Versailles "dic- tate" had given the victors, the satiated powers, twinges of

belated conscience over their vindictive peace. Prior to Herr
Hitler, conquest for imperial purposes inside Europe had been
mostly confined to adjustments within the Balkan peninsula,
or a few relatively unimportant plebiscites for restoration of
small portions of territory taken in previous wars. In general,
the mind of the world was apparently adjusted to the idea that
territorial problems in Europe itself would hardly be solved
by conquest or any other form of unilateral activity. Empires were overseas adjuncts to power, prestige, or "home"
resources. Allotment of these, although grossly unequal, followed a roughly appreciated international comity, posited for
the most part upon the accepted naval dominance of Great
Britain in alliance with France through this century.

But with the progress of Nazi revindication all this changed.
The established practices of diplomacy failed, international
law was swept aside, treaties had only kaleidoscopic validity,
and additions to the German Reich have been entirely by unilateral action, essentially in violation of the postwar World
Constitution. At the beginning, each coup d'état was con-
doned by the fact that injustices within the Versailles treaty,
owing to the implacable enmity of England and France, had
as yet prevented collective solution of the needs of the German
Reich. These needs included full parity in armaments and
access to colonial products, and to markets, which would restore to Germany the full sovereignty which she had once
enjoyed. But in the process of this readjustment the idea of
restoration of population and territory became obscured, and
the question of raw products grew to larger proportions, en-
tailing control of the balance of political power and economic

and political domination of Europe, which would, if successful, relegate the hitherto successful imperialistic powers to a
secondary place. In this process the balance has shifted from
West to East, leaving the democratic states dependent upon
overseas possessions and Dominions, leaving Italy to rely upon
her wits as a possible ally of one side or the other, and Germany at last dependent upon the good will of Russia. For the
moment, at least, the fate of Europe lies in the hands of Asia,
as it has not since Vienna was liberated from the Ottoman
threat in 1683 by John Sobieski, the patriot king of Poland.

*The ever-increasing tension of the imperialistic philoso-
phies.*—As this problem draws into its web all parts of the
world, it is no longer pertinent to speak of the present critical
situation as one of the "wars of Europe." If we examine the
intensification of overseas imperialism from its inception to
its present Frankenstein menace, it becomes evident that the
American world is part and parcel of the system, is indeed
both its creature and its creator; and the idea that we have
no concern with the most recent quarrels of Europe is a denial
of historic processes, or a misinterpretation of the actualities,
full of the danger implicit in an unjustified break with the
past. I speak of this not merely for the joy of belaboring the
obvious, but to try to show that any solution of the problems
of imperialism must have a great effect on the United States,
and not only that we have a responsibility toward the solution,
but that our very existence is inherent in both process and
outcome.

There has been no moment in the history of the expansion
of Europe when the tensions between the neighbor nations

were not as great as the national organization and the political ambitions of the moment could bear, and releases of such tensions have always affected America. When the nations of Christendom began to emigrate from the seagirt shores of Western Europe, each of them was moved by the sentiment that all the others were foreign, and hence suspect; but they were united in the ties of a common faith, which was the essential unity of Christendom, against which they set the outer darkness of Paganism. This apparent unity in disunity had been reached by opportune recognition by national kings at various times of the temporal overheadship of the Catholic Church, which had made its way to influence by seizing upon the rivalries of national dynasties, and which stood for the moment as international arbiter over those parts of the extra-European world which were to be brought within the fold of Christendom through the continued activities of church and state.

The international authority of the pope was the only such authority in existence, although the Holy Roman Empire undertook to impose a similar idea. The partition of the new discoveries in the bulls of Alexander VI was an essay toward acceptance of an established international authority, but was, unfortunately, a monument to geographical ignorance rather than to impartial arbitrament, and subsisted for only a brief year, 1493–1494, when in the Treaty of Tordesillas the two rival Iberian states undertook to decide for themselves, without papal sanction, those problems which had been imperfectly envisaged under the bulls. From that moment, the rivalry of Spain and Portugal attained a new acerbity with

the mutually suspicious partitioning of the pagan world until, toward the end of the century, their monopoly was broken
by the rise of the parvenu countries, England, France, and
Holland, each denying the validity of prior international partition and challenging the monopolists upon the basis of discovery and occupation. The expansion of Europe was thus a
prime cause of the failure to attain European unity, and let
loose two hundred years of wars between mutually destruc-
tive nationalisms, which, in this current crisis, constitute the
direst threat to the continuance of European political society.

Within each of these 16th-century nation-states, the provi-
sion of revenues with which to pay for centralization was to
come from the mercantile interest involved in the discovery
and occupation of extra-European areas. The Crown, in each
state, either became identified with the mercantile interests
or depended upon them as the chief bulwark of national
strength. The philosophy of mercantilism thus developed, so
far as each competitor was confronted with his rival, meant
that the prosperity of any state was inimical to that of each
and every other. Mercantilism thus spread beyond the confines of Europe in the form of monopoly, heritage of the
Middle Ages, as the basic principle of social evolution, economic power, and political prestige. In the exterminative
policies of the totalitarians, the neo-mercantilism of the 19th
century attains its 20th-century apotheosis.

Politically, the idea of national sovereignty kept pace with
that of economic evolution. The 16th-century rift with the
Church widened national rivalries. Most of the causes of old
wars were transmuted into colonial causes and were so trans-

mitted to the oceans and new-found lands overseas. Modified by geography and the rising national spirit, mercantilism was one of the chief agencies whereby international tensions became innate in the life of the New World until they were crushed by the great 17th-century contraband trade. Colonial possessions were established in most of the temperate regions of the unoccupied world, coast lines were divided among the colonizing powers, and their hinterlands were staked out as areas of prospective occupation. In the 18th century, national rivalries continued, with here the elimination of Danish and Swedish, there the elimination of Dutch and French, until the British Empire emerged triumphant, confronted only by the widely spread but weakened Spaniards.

The same century saw next the emancipation of the British colonies and the beginning of emancipation for those of Spain. While political independence appeared as the visible good, it was the fight for economic independence that had the chief and most dramatic import. The absence or default of the personal sovereign facilitated growth of the idea of sovereignty residing in a whole population, that is, the evolution of a sort of democracy spreading over continental areas, a democracy not yet entirely operative anywhere, but developing in the present century in a variety of types throughout the Americas and finding counterparts in China and the Near East. In the newborn United States, interest shifted quickly to a struggle to retain all the commercial advantages of the earlier membership in the British Empire; and this contest has continuously increased in intensity with the advent of the technological age. The century closed upon the failure of

Napoleon I to destroy the predominance of England, to dictate the forms of political existence in Europe, and to control the resources of the dependent areas of the extra-European world.

The Napoleonic struggle was marked by a change in degree rather than in kind from the tensions developed during the 17th century. The extra-European world had assumed greater importance with the passage of time; and the successes of England, apparently made dominant through overseas possessions, aroused the Napoleonic impulse to wrest India, Africa, and America from the hated England, "the wart always under our nose."

A new epoch of overseas enterprise opened with the beginnings of the French conquest of Algeria, although South Africa had appeared as a British possession even before Napoleon had passed. There followed these episodes a new swarm of scientific voyages similar to those of the late 18th century, missionary enterprises renewed upon the ideals of conflicting Catholic and Protestant ambitions, and increase of trade due to the development of the steamship and of factory methods. Germany and Italy, emergent as unified states with rounded-out European possessions, showed an immediate thirst for overseas empire with which they might emulate the successes of the British and the French. In another two decades, the United States and Japan, with ambitions for new worlds to conquer, entered the competition, and the tension of imperial rivalry was increased by the number of participants in the strife, the development of overseas trade, and the lessening of the areas in the extra-European world that were susceptible to European occupation. When technological mass production exceeded the national markets, or when capital sought adventures overseas to earn going rates of interest, national rivalries grew. These in turn, beginning in the 1870's and 1880's, made imperative the seizure of protectorates, spheres of influence or of interest, to monopolize markets and raw products for the nation at the expense of rivals. If I have made my point, it is clear that, once international arbitrament had been thrust aside, the course of national imperialism drove ever forward in a series of tensions and explosions, in which the Great War and its faulty peace were episodic and characteristic but not determinative of any real change in psychological attitude toward the causes of wars.

Preliminaries of the Great War.—The habit which evolved during the closing years of the 19th century, of convoking the powers for the purposes of settling various world problems, proved how serious were the conflicts of interest. From the Berlin Conference of 1878, concerned with Levantine problems, and the Madrid Conference of 1880, down to and including all the subsequent efforts for the adjustment of the African partitions, it became increasingly evident that the uncertain shifts of power politics showed the impractibility of the balance of power to secure any durable peace. Yet there was a semblance of good faith in negotiations. The Bismarckian period was cold and ruthless, but the Iron Chancellor knew the worth of the bones of a Pomeranian grenadier, and governed his policies in the light of the enduring values. But with colonial expansion and industrialization came inevitably the notion that resources for technical advancement would yield the ascendancy in time of war, which loomed more imminent with every intrusion into a coveted dependent area, and with each improvement of weapons of offense or defense.

Nor should we forget that in the creation and solution of these problems the United States early took a consequential part. It would be to the point to show that each episode in the wars by which America was partitioned, say from 1688 to 1763, was part and parcel of the process cumulating in 1914–1918 and 1933–1939; but there is not time for such a recital. Passing by as perhaps embryonic the acts of the United States with regard to the opening of China and Japan and the establishment of American contacts with Africa in Liberia, we must recall that our country intervened in European affairs in the Madrid Conference of 1880, concerning the problems of the protégés (forerunner of later attempts to partition Morocco). It was in something of a missionary attitude, or at least with no essential business interests at stake, that the American Senate ratified without reservation this purely Afro-European agreement. Furthermore, our share in the Hague conventions was essentially interference in Europe, our real fears of naval armament being platonic rather than real.

When the Moroccan question had become, through the celebration of the Entente Cordiale (1904) by France and England, a challenge to the political prestige of Germany, Roosevelt, in his pursuit of *Machtpolitik,* undertook to meddle in the situation, demanding the bandit Raisuli dead or alive. This was perhaps mere showmanship, at least a personal executive reaction to foreign stimulus for dramatic effect. Once again Theodore Roosevelt espoused the idea of an international convention when he supported Germany's demand for an international conference when the French preferred not to have one over the subject of Morocco. The Act of Algeciras, of April 7, 1906, was signed by the plenipotentiary of the United States. The Senate ratified the Act with reservations, and it remains today one of the ways through which our intervention in the coming African partition may happen. Under conceivable circumstances, we may not be able to avoid intrusion there.

The same Roosevelt in 1905 had intervened to bring peace between Russia and Japan in the Treaty of Portsmouth, in an effort to add one more continent to American prestige. In later crises in Morocco the intervention of the United States was lacking, as it had been in the Balkan crises. The feeling of caution which swept over the American Senate in 1899 has developed into a check of the legislative branch upon the executive in international negotiations, which has tended to weaken the efficacy of our government in the conduct of foreign relations. It is unnecessary to recall to this audience the details of the struggle for power in the Levant immediately prior to the Sarajevo incident. Let it suffice, therefore, to recall that the balance of power method had, by the opening of the World War, found the nations of Europe divided into two opposing systems of alliance, the Triple Entente and the Triple Alliance, and had developed such bitterness that, as the best thing which imperialism had to offer to the solution of conflicting ambitions, it proved unequal to its task.

The abysmal ignorance with which the United States saw

that war begin and develop, together with our devious behavior during and after it, demonstrated how little we understood our identity with the processes of imperialism and
our joint responsibility, together with the other expansionist
states, for its operation. Our participation in that war has been
characterized as a mistaken meddling, but it has not been
shown that it was not a natural result of the process through
which came our origins and our evolution. We are now
again able to imagine what the results of Allied defeat might
have meant. Nor may we escape the logic of the current shifts
of the system of world balance, unless we assume our reasonable share in its control or modification.

Development of a world organization.—During the prose-
cution of the Great War, while the philosophy of Woodrow
Wilson dominated political thought, lip service at least was
given to the idea of framing a world constitution which would
relegate to the past the deceits and treacheries of pre-War
diplomacy and the threadbare pretenses of the balances of
power. In the Covenant of the League of Nations there
emerged a system of world organization which, had it been
actually and sincerely applied, would have eliminated major
frictions of national sovereignty and exploitation of resources.
Henceforth there were to be rules of the game, serving as a
guide to political actions between rivals. Furthermore, the
Covenant provided reasonably adequate means for the pro-
gressive revision of those among its own terms which might
in the course of experience prove unworkable. It was a system,
however, which contemplated the adhesion of all civilized
states and a universal affirmative will to use it so as to elim-

inate the causes of friction which had brought about the great disintegration. So sharp was the break with the habits of power politics, and so ideal were the desired ends of universal peace, that the League proved to be an unrealizable abstraction, while the inequalities of the nations and of their control of natural resources made the new Constitution in the eyes of Germans and other "revisionists" appear to be a sanctification of injustice and a perpetuation of inequality.

Gradual disintegration of the League was caused, moreover, by the course of events which ensued immediately upon the presentation of the Peace Treaties and the Covenant to the world powers for ratification. In the first place, the United States, whose president was chief author of the idea, utterly rejected the League and the ideals of world coöperation. That was internal and personal politics plus the ennui developed by reaction to long emotional strain. It was followed a few years later by our rejection of the Court of International Justice, once again a curious American denial of an American ideal, a surprise to the entire country brought about by isolationist senators thinking in pre-War frames of reference.

Furthermore, in actual operation the League was utilized by the victorious powers as an adjunct and auxiliary to their earlier methods of manipulating European affairs through balances, rather than as a substitute for and reform of the old system. By using the League for solution of minor problems the great powers seemed to maintain the new ideal, but in the larger issues they reverted to the practices of *Machtpolitik*. In pursuit of this dual method, France was animated by her ancient fear of invasion by Germany, and Great Britain by her jealousy lest France, with her great army, should, in pursuit of "security," assume an entire hegemony of Europe, leaving England as a peripheral power. Both states were indifferent to the success of the Weimar Republic, gave equivocal support to the economic welfare of Austria, and repeatedly evaded reduction of armaments to conform with the limitation which had been imposed upon Germany. At the same time, other "revisionists" sought relief from economic depression by blaming others for their own misfortunes. It was inevitable, then, that there should be a recurrent defection of powers injured by or disciplined by a world organization which achieved only moderate success. Inherent in the breakdown was the fact that the application of sanctions to an aggressor state could not be made adequately by League forces, since none existed, or by economic or military intervention of the powerful states if the sanction indicated did not conserve their particular national interests. Thus the regional pacts, which had been used to augment the security sought in collective action, had no greater validity than the pre-War treaties which had permitted recurrent shifts of the balance of power. We are familiar with the externals at least of the defection of Japan and Germany and the flaunting of the League by Italy. It is now beside the point to repeat the rationalizations by which those states determined upon violation of their international promises. One more broad fact here calls for iteration, and that is that had American support of the League been followed by Europe in 1931, the path to improvement in world relations would probably have remained open.

We must not neglect, however, the fact that the establishment of a proletarian regime in Russia, and that country's determination to rouse a world-wide Marxian revolution, frightened the imperial powers with a dread of internal economic breakdown in the spread of Communism. The almost incessant snubbing of Russia in recent years may prove as unwise as France's attitude toward Germany in the decade 1904-1914. Again, the lesser powers had in turn contributed their own share to the inapplicability of the League ideal by their repeated insistence that the great powers should support various smaller states in international conflicts in which the interests of the great states were remote. This was especially true of the situations in which the British navy might have been called upon to enforce the dicta of the League.

There was, then, even within the period of the political respectability of the League, a gradual return to the spirit of the balance of power. Since the Manchurian violation of 1931, the methods of collective security have had no courageous backers; since Munich, the League has received blow after blow until it is practically dead as a political force. It may even be asserted that by their control of capital and labor, their emphasis on rearmament, their secret police, and their racial and political purges the totalitarian states have dealt to world organization the coup de grace; they have passed beyond the old standards of capitalism and imperialism, opening a new and epochal threat to any hope of creating a world society. This shift became vividly apparent shortly before the September declarations of war upon Germany by Britain and France. If totalitarian aims are successful, they preclude any balance of power, but provide for the unstable dominance of a self-selected power or group of powers, with instability and recurrent seizures as their terroristic methods of influence. While such a system prevails, all the ordinary processes of international life are at a standstill.

Such, then, is the result of the system which the imperial states have imposed upon themselves. J. A. Hobson concludes his *Imperialism, A Study* (1902) with the following characterization of the process: "Imperialism is a depraved choice of national life, imposed by self-seeking interests which appeal to the lusts of quantitative acquisitiveness and forceful domination surviving in a nation from early centuries of animal struggle for existence. Its adoption as a policy implies a deliberate renunciation of that cultivation of the higher inner qualities which for a nation as for an individual constitutes the ascendancy of reason over brute impulse. It is the besetting sin of all successful states, and its penalty is unalterable in the order of nature." In a newer work Hobson has confessed himself an economic heretic, but two recent critics have called his book "the most seminal work on economic imperialism."

It is thus obvious that the imperial solution has proved historically to be *The Great Illusion* which Norman Angell called it a quarter-century ago. It must also be elementary that in the present crisis of imperialism the Allied purpose to remove Hitlerism and the menace of Germany to the other states of Europe is not enough; the war must be pursued to the point where even the imperialism of the states which declare they are defending the liberties of Europe must retrace the path of their errors and ignorance, both since 1919 and before, and turn their wills to the task of making the world safe for all the peoples who live in it. Any American pretense of indifference toward the realization of such a task is simple denial of reality.

The mandates.—The League experiment for control of dependent areas suffered from similar constitutional defects and shortcomings in operation. Yet it was of a kind with the anti-imperial movement of this century which evolved the British Dominions, set Cuba free, cut certain Balkan and Arabic states from the Turkish Empire, progressed to self-determination for a number of central European entities, and brought to an end extraterritoriality in Egypt, Siam, and the Orient.

The basic principle of Article 22 of the Covenant, creating the Permanent Mandates Commission, was that the administration of backward peoples is a trust for their benefit, the terms of which must be fixed and regulated by international law, and that the process should eventuate in independence. The mandate system sanctioned a prior distribution, by secret agreement among the great powers, of the colonies taken from Germany and Turkey. This was done by an elaboration of the war-guilt reasoning, in which the League made a virtue of necessity by sanctioning the grabs of the powers. The Mandates Commission received functions of supervision and regulation beyond its power to enforce against unwilling mandatories. The severed parts of the Turkish Empire, presumably nearly ready for independence, which was in effect assured to them, were designated as Class A mandates; those considered capable of ultimately reaching independence were

the German territories, in which there was a considerable social evolution and some economic value, the B mandates. Class
C was the residue, and constituted areas which were not conceivably capable of attaining sovereign capacities. They were
expected to be assimilated practically to the status of constit-
uent parts of the colonial realms of the recipient mandatories.

The Mandates Commission's members were chosen from
among the victorious powers, the defeated ones having no
representation. The commission was theoretically to enforce
the provisions of the League for the government of the mandates. Over each of the latter an official not connected with the
colonial empire of the mandatory was to enforce the legislation which was intended to make the mandates system superior to any hitherto developed colonial fabric. It was, in fact,
an elaboration of the idea of "trusteeship" by which the British
consider that they have mitigated the harshness of the impact
of the higher civilization upon the weaker. While this judgment is not fully shared by impartial critics, it seems to have
worked better in certain respects than the system of "association" which the French evolved for the indirect rule of native
societies. For the benefit of trade, the open door was to be the
principle ensuring equality among commercial nations.

As their story has evolved, the only mandate which has
achieved a constructive independence has been Iraq under the
British (1932). Next to it are the various parts of the mandate
known as Syria, which comprises four or five entities of varying political stature and approaches closely the status of Iraq,
but which, owing to complications greater than those of the
British area, still lags on the journey toward sovereignty. As

a matter of fact, because of their geographical situation, their social characteristics, and their strategic value, there is not much present prospect that the mandates of Iraq and Syria will early attain the stature of free and independent states. The same observations are true of all classes of mandates, as indeed they are of many simple colonies.

The attitudes assumed in recent years by the unsatiated states, in their philosophies of racial superiority, absolute sovereignty, and unilateral decisions hostile to the spirit of the mandates system, have destroyed confidence in the success of the humanitarian and liberal principles, and even the Permanent Mandates Commission questions the likelihood of the spread of these principles to other backward peoples. In addition to the repeated troubles of the French in Syria, those of the British in Palestine have attracted world-wide interest. The hard fate of the Jews in the face of British struggles to find an adequate solution of the question of partition, shows how much patience and skill would be needed to make progress in self-government in areas of mutually hostile populations. For the French, the alienation to Turkey of Alexandretta stirred old flames of Syrian anger.

One of the troubles which have confronted the operation of the other mandates has been the difficulty of ascertaining what citizenship the inhabitants possess. Obviously it is not that of the mandates; and it is not possibly that of the League, which is not a state in the usual acceptance of the term. How, then, can such entities rid themselves of tutelage and evolve independently? For an appreciable time the operation of the Mandates Commission served to ameliorate the condition of the mandated natives, inasmuch as the reports of each entity, by becoming public property for those who cared to see them, reduced abuses in labor relations, military service, and justice, abuses which were, unfortunately, common in colonial areas under the imperial regime.

Amelioration of labor conditions was brought about, in large part, through the functioning of the International Labor Office, which undertook to set forth, on paper at least, working conditions intended to conserve the health of individuals, and specifications for sanitary arrangements upon public and private works of large proportions, to which the natives might not be transported to long distances from their homes. All camps of forced laborers were to have frequent sanitary inspections, and physical examinations should further conserve the labor supply. So far as voicing the grievances of mandated peoples was concerned, the efficacy of the League Commission was less than had been expected because of the reluctance with which mandatory powers heeded or admitted complaints as offered. These were often alleged to be the product of Communistic propaganda or the outcries of irrational nationalistic groups within the mandated areas, and were ignored.

Perhaps one of the most essential difficulties of the operation of the mandates has been the burden placed upon a mandatory power to supply the required hygienic, sanitary, and educational necessities of the natives. Yet the work in the mandates within Africa and that of New Zealand has more recently progressed with less criticism than arose during their first decade. The retention of the Caroline Islands by Japan proved that for nations that have given up League membership the legal right to the mandated territory reposes in the mandatories of the imperial regime rather than under the sanction of League bestowal. Japanese refusal to coöperate by accrediting a representative to the Commission since the League invoked sanctions in the war in China has raised the legal question of the validity of Japanese tenure of the North Pacific islands.

Another feature of mandate operation was that natives enlisted in the armed forces of the mandatory might not be utilized for other than police service, and within the area of their habitat. There was a certain degree of fatuousness in this regulation, inasmuch as the habitat of a tribe is rarely as large as the mandated territory, so that the rule might be observed in law although violated in spirit by moving enlisted or conscripted groups out of their immediate tribal stamping grounds. As a matter of fact, in the territories given to France as Class B mandates, regulations were, if general report is to be believed, frequently violated, as the French did not refrain from moving Negro troops in accordance with current needs for the utilization of armed forces of blacks, regardless of the inhibition. Exigencies of empire, in fact, required frequently that black troops should be used for preserving the peace of North Africa, where local troops were not to be trusted when the occasion might arise for quelling uprisings. The rule that a Mohammedan may not kill a Mohammedan was of greater practical result in the management of the French empire than the rules governing League mandates.

Another feature which has presented difficulties has been the question of the duration of the mandates within the B class. There was for several years an agitation for the development within the British Empire of an East African union in such a form as to preclude the possibility of the return of Tanganyika to the Germans. With respect to all the mandates in Africa, the outcry of the totalitarian powers, particularly of Germany for the return of her colonies, has been posited upon the idea of *Lebensraum* and upon the return of raw-products supply areas. The whole argument presupposes wartime difficulty in obtaining essential supplies, and upon the fallacy that tropical regions can be made areas of expansion for white populations. Moreover, the open-door policy as employed in Africa has not really opened trade opportunities to the unsatiated powers, and variations of currencies used in exchange have served to further canalize the trade of the mandatory.

Perhaps the worst fault of the mandates idea was that it included only the colonies of the vanquished states. Not even the areas within the Conventional Basin of the Congo (largely in Allied hands) were included, though these had been neutralized, and were mostly suitable for inclusion within the mandates idea. Moreover, areas apparently internationalized as mandates are too small and too widely separated to relieve needs for raw products, war materials, or transfers of populations. Where conquest changes the status of European countries, as is now occurring, the imposition of mandate control would be as unreasonable as imperialism in the raw.

Since the Great War, the movement in the colonial world has been toward realization of the seriousness of the problem of the backward populations and of the need of meeting German and Italian demands for colonies. It was even suggested by a Britisher that some territory now held by Great Britain should be ceded to a refurbished League and that other countries should be induced to make similar cessions. Nothing of the sort has yet happened. At the moment no shift of colonial territory is imminent, but settlement awaits the end of the war. If my thesis has any validity, the war must end with the victory of the western powers, and the reconstitution of a League of Nations ready and willing to enforce sanctions and to take under its direct control all dependent areas of the world which are incapable of self-development and some measure of self-defense and yet are of strategic value or are coveted for their economic resources. To bring this about, a new League, agreed upon and accepted by all as a superstate, must bestow territory and develop trade relations with due attention to the needs of all the several powers upon a peace footing. There can be no monopoly of war resources, no hinterland furnishing sinews of war to some monopolistic tyrant, no class-conscious proletariat or purse-proud investor, no exploitation of the weak by the strong. In a word, imperialism must legislate itself out of existence.

Admittedly, there is no prospect of such an outcome of the present hypertension. None of the movements now possible—not the once-feared alliance of the anti-Comintern states; not Mr. Clarence Streit's *Union Now* for the democracies, nor our tender affection for Latin America, evolved from our fear of encroaching totalitarianism; not even our well-nigh hysterical unanimity to remain innocent bystanders in the war while abjuring none of the anticipated blessings of an Allied victory; not even the declared aims of the Allies themselves—seems to offer hope of such a categorical denouement. Our international quandary comes from long obedience to the elementary urges of pugnacity, prestige, and predacity. When perhaps another blood bath convinces us that such a course is inane, we may revert to milder uses of the instinct of self-preservation as a mandate from an empire yet remote from our present jangled existence.

THE RELATION
BETWEEN INTERNATIONAL TRADE
AND PEACE

———

ROBERT D. CALKINS
DEAN OF THE COLLEGE OF COMMERCE
IN THE UNIVERSITY OF CALIFORNIA

Lecture delivered October 31, 1939

THE RELATION
BETWEEN INTERNATIONAL TRADE
AND PEACE

T HE AUTARCHY, treaty violations, economic warfare, territorial expansion, and armed conflict of the last decade
constitute a major threat to the power, prestige, and prosperity
of the established order of great powers and to the political
and economic foundations on which these things rest. Appeasement by surrender has not been notably successful in
reducing the hazards to those who have most to lose. Since
some, though by no means all, of the conditions producing
this impasse are economic in character, it has been proposed,
especially by the United States, that international trade may
offer a peaceful solution of the economic deficiencies of the
unsatiated and densely populated states. This solution, it is
contended, makes necessary no redrawing of boundaries, no
extension of sovereignty, no war of aggression. A general revision of international economic policies to free the channels
of trade and to promote international economic coöperation
is sufficient, and the expansion of trade, the restoration of prosperity, and the establishment of a prolonged if not a permanent peace would, it is argued, result.

If such proposals, coming belatedly from nations with commercial empires, are treated with suspicion or disinterest by
those who have begun the redistribution of world power, prestige, and resources, it is understandable. Even though the proposal be fundamentally sound, one is not wholly irrational to

doubt its practicability in achieving prosperity and peace in a world where prestige and power may currently be regarded as more important than either peace or prosperity. Moreover, after examining the history of foreign policy, one may legitimately doubt the political ability of nations to supply the necessary coöperation and tolerance for success.

It is my object to consider this proposal with special reference to its fundamental validity and practicability. The fact that war has begun will not lessen the pertinence of the inquiry, for, whatever the outcome of the present conflict, the task of economic reconstruction will inevitably postulate the choice between some form of world economic system or an alternative economic structure. The decision is not one for victorious statesmen alone, for it will vitally affect all nations, including our own. Let us not misunderstand: the alternative of reconstructing a world economy does not mean a return to the prewar internationalism which was abandoned in 1914. Whatever system is adopted, whether truly international or one of self-sufficient economic blocs, it must be adjusted to the technological and structural changes in economic affairs which are not reversible and which prevent a return to the past.

To understand the fundamental role of trade in modern society, one must start with two realities: the geographical distribution of population, having varied wants to be satisfied; and the geographical distribution of the resources which are capable of satisfying the wants. The economic problem presented by these realities is that of most effectively utilizing such scarce resources as the world possesses for the maximum satisfaction of human wants. The first principle of elementary economics emphasizes the gains in economic welfare which are possible through the division of human labor and the geographical specialization of production. But a necessary corollary of specialization in production is trade by which regions and individuals may obtain the variety of goods and services they need in exchange for the specialized products they produce. An inevitable result of territorial specialization and trade is economic interdependence in which the welfare of all rests upon the continuity and coördination of the specialized economic activities.

Since the beginning of the commercial revolution, the world has shown a remarkable ingenuity in pursuing the advantages of territorial specialization. In the century of great economic progress just before the World War, the standard of living rose for most of the world more rapidly than in any comparable period theretofore of which we have knowledge. The phenomenal growth of population which accompanied the improvement of economic welfare emphasizes the magnitude of the achievement. The explanation is to be found in two main lines of development: first, industrialization, facilitated by new sources of power and technical improvements in machines and processes; and second, territorial specialization and trade, which utilized resources of all accessible regions and made them available where needed by means of improved transport facilities. Territorial specialization and trade within national boundaries were only part of this expansion. International specialization was deliberately encouraged through the policies of imperialism and comparative freedom in trade.

Between 1850 and 1913 the volume of international trade increased tenfold.[1]

In this period of industrialization no nation escaped the integration of its own economic activities with those of other nations. It is no exaggeration to say that by 1914 we had achieved an interdependent world economy. International trade had become a vital and essential part of the economic process by which the people of all nations lived. On this account the destruction of trade had become an increasingly important military objective in wartime and its control a political objective in peacetime.

During the past quarter-century, the retreat from internationalism has conflicted everywhere with the economic interdependence achieved and the further interdependence required for economic stability and prosperity. The sporadic attempts at economic reconstruction in the decade of the 'twenties temporarily stabilized currencies, partly reduced trade restrictions, and restored international lending. The result was a poorly grounded and hurriedly erected economic reconstruction, a return to prosperity and a revival of international trade to an all-time peak in 1929. But with the depression came a desperate resort to nationalistic remedies for domestic and international problems alike. International collaboration, which had been difficult in the 'twenties, became virtually impossible in the 'thirties. The weakened position of the League of Nations, the spectacular collapse of the London Economic Conference in 1933 and of the World Disarmament

---

[1] B. Ohlin, *International Economic Reconstruction* (Paris, Chamber of Commerce, 1936), p. 29.

Conference in 1934, were only symptomatic. With the collapse of voluntary international coöperation, protective self-sufficiency programs spread; isolation was sought by some states; others resorted to international coercion.

We are living under new conditions, but the basic economic problem remains the same. It is that of organizing for the most effective use of the scarce resources of the world. It is a world problem, and as long as we have autonomous states it is an international one and must be solved by international coöperation. Therefore, before we relegate the era of international economics to the history books and look back on the good old days with historical homesickness, let us take inventory and consider again the attempt to solve this economic problem by means of international trade.

Pre-War trade and imperialism.—An empirical and popular conclusion often drawn from historical experience with world trade is that it has not produced peace in the past and cannot be expected to do so in the future. The popularity of the conclusion is itself a sufficient reason for analyzing the evidence.

Two views regarding the coercive implications of trade provide the basis for most arguments about its effects on peace. One is that trade is fundamentally a voluntary and peaceful activity, mutually beneficial, and requiring peaceful conditions for its greatest benefits and full development. The other is that trade is also, or instead, acquisitive, exploitative, and predatory and leads to coercion of the weak by the strong. The view that trade is fundamentally peaceful has been widely accepted since the spread of classical economics. The view that it is coercive and exploitative, at least in capitalistic systems, predominates among the critics of capitalism. That trade may be of either type, depending on the tolerance, selfishness, and mores of the traders is obvious. Numerous historical examples of both types of trade could be cited, but whatever the dominant practice in a given period, it is usually punctuated with instances of the contrary sort.

Since the policies of national states reflect in varying degrees the interests of nationals, such policies quite naturally become adjusted to economic interests, among others. At times they reflect the economic interests of special groups having influence. To the extent that traders, then, seek commercial opportunities and advantages in foreign territory through the instrument of governmental policy and pressure, trade may be regarded as one motive for imperialism. The pressure is less direct, but the motive is fundamentally the same, if nations follow imperialistic practices not at the request of business interests, but, instead, under the influence of currently accepted ideologies of economic expansion by force. The use of coercion or force to achieve territorial expansion, political domination, and economic concessions for purposes of economic exploitation or development frequently leads directly to war. Such actions also may deprive independent peoples of vital economic opportunities, stimulate a preference for defensive aggression, and eventually destroy the peace.

War and imperialism, as acquisitive political activities, may spring from other than economic motives, however. Imperialism, by which we mean the use of coercion and force to dominate independent states and territories, may be, and in fact has been, pursued for reasons of pride, prestige, power, and religion. Until modern times, such motives, together with plunder and tribute, were important reasons for war and empire building. Such objectives as plunder, slaves, and tribute in ancient wars were of course economic in character. Only as trading became more profitable than wars for plunder and tribute did the character of the economic motive and economic organization shift to its modern counterpart. But it was not until after the great discoveries and the improvement of transportation that trade furnished the dominant motives and objectives for imperialistic policy and war. The most notable growth of the economic motive has occurred since the 15th century. The course of imperialism and war since that time has been so intimately interwoven with trade expansion that the historian instinctively looks for economic motives, and rarely has difficulty in finding some. Nevertheless, it is recognized that noneconomic motives are usually necessary for the existence of imperialism, and that in many such ventures the economic motives were not dominant.

The great trading companies of Europe, armed with monopoly privilege and broad powers, initially were concerned with trade and profits rather than territorial possessions. When these opportunities were insufficient, piracy, plunder, and territorial conquest ensued.[2] Colonial expansion in the Western Hemisphere is a well-known illustration of such conquest and conflict, first for the possession of territory and later for its redivision among ambitious European powers. The overseas

---

[2] M. J. Bonn, *The Crumbling of Empire* (London, Allen & Unwin, 1938), pp. 33–37.

expansion was much the same everywhere down to the wars of independence at the turn of the 18th century.

In this expansion the desire for national power was no doubt as influential a motive as economic advantage. It should be noted, however, that the policy of conducting trade under conditions of monopoly, privilege, and strict regulation drove maritime nations in self-protection to enter the field aggressively. To share in the direct benefits of trade, overseas expansion was considered necessary, and territory was prized both for its importance to one's trading empire and for its appropriation against rivals.

As the advantages of freer trade grew, and Manchester economics provided the rationale for abandoning mercantilistic regulation, the necessity for overseas empire was lessened. The wars of independence arose in no small measure from the desire to throw off the restrictions which current commercial policy imposed on trade.

Freeing domestic and international trade from regulation in the 19th century was a major step, first, in unifying nations, and then in the creation of a world economy among independent states and empires. But the rapid development of industry soon exhausted markets, and the search for resources, markets, and overseas investment opportunities started the final intensified scramble for undeveloped territory in weak hands. France and England resumed the expansion of their empires. By the end of the century the partition of Africa was almost complete. Germany and Italy entered the race late, but nevertheless got a foothold in Africa in the final decades. The end of the century found the English, French, Germans, and

Russians with significant holdings in Asia, and virtually all of Polynesia in European hands.

Imperialistic economic motives were characteristic of these ventures. Upon taking Tunisia in 1881, the French frankly admitted that it was necessary as a market and a profitable field for investment. Joseph Chamberlain could say with pride that "commerce is the greatest of all political interests." The United States was not above acquiring Puerto Rico or the Philippines. Nor was Theodore Roosevelt exactly pacifistic in wielding the Big Stick. The final scramble for concessions and territorial crumbs was competitive to the degree that France and Great Britain jointly were on the verge of war because a German gunboat anchored off the Moroccan coast in 1911 and threatened their imperialistic plans.

Whether this great territorial expansion was achieved by peaceful conquest or by armed conflict, it was in any case deliberate and coercive, and somewhere in the background of motives was the desire for markets, resources, and power in the race of expanding empires. In the century before 1914 the spread of the free-trade argument had brought by one means or another a general reduction, if not abandonment, of restrictive commercial regulations. International trade expanded to new heights and no nation was exempt, willingly or unwillingly, from the benefits and obligations of economic internationalism. It was now possible to cite examples of prosperity through trade without empire. The cost of modern warfare and the appropriation, by comparatively strong powers, of most of the earth's surface on all continents increased greatly the cost of further empire building. Moreover, colonial expansion had not been the economic success that was hoped. Germany's annual imports from her possessions before the war amounted to only about 13 million dollars, while in contrast her imports from the United States amounted to about 345 million dollars.[3] Her raw material imports from colonies were merely 1 per cent of the total. Nor had any great migration occurred. All Germans living in her colonies amounted to only half their number in the Bronx, the New York borough having the fewest Germans. Over a ten-year period the total trade with her colonies amounted to less than a billion marks, while the colonial expenses in the period exceeded this figure.[4] What was true of the German case was duplicated in others. In brief, most of the colonial empires which had been built up had become more important for prestige and power than for resources or markets.

As one reviews this period of trade expansion, it becomes clear that desire for trade and profit did furnish a powerful motive for political imperialism and war. It is also clear that imperialistic expansion once begun encouraged others to enter the race, and that, because of the restrictive commercial policies followed, only limited trade and benefits were possible for a nation which did not expand its own commerce and empire. Thus, for profit, protection, pride, prestige, and power the European nations extended their sovereignty to every continent on earth. Only with the relaxation of trade restrictions, begun in the last century, was a basis laid for making further

---

[3] H. F. Frazer, *Foreign Trade and World Politics* (London, Knopf, 1927), p. 116.

[4] Grover Clark, *The Balance Sheet of Imperialism* (New York, Columbia University Press, 1936), pp. 10–11.

empire building economically unnecessary. With the political and economic frontiers pushed approximately to their geographical limits, the world seemed in 1914 to be nearing the end of an era. The economic task ahead was mainly that of developing commercial and foreign policy so as to make the most of world resources in an existing world economy, and to remove economic friction as a cause of war. But such questions received scant attention in the current concern with power politics. As the war progressed and the campaign against shipping and trade was extended, the problems of economic mobilization were the pressing issues. Upon the conclusion of hostilities, nothing seemed quite so important as the transition to a peacetime economy and the reconstruction of Europe; larger questions which were to provide the basis for avoiding the next war were necessarily delayed.

Post-War policy.—The return of peace brought some prospect that formal international coöperation might at last be achieved through the organization of the League of Nations. There was even promise that some degree of political stability, or orderly change, among the nations would be possible. This would have been a first step toward solving the problem of international economic welfare. But the peace treaty laid an inadequate foundation for an enduring economic peace. The League was less effective than had been hoped. To the mistakes of the Treaty of Versailles were added more important mistakes of international and domestic economic policy, which greatly prolonged necessary readjustments and created further maladjustments for all. The post-War policy of France and Britain has reflected many of these mistakes and an unwillingness to meet the larger issues. The attempt of the United States to claim the benefits of a creditor position in a world economy without assuming the costs and responsibilities was one of the early and crucial mistakes in the series. From our policy flowed much, though by no means all, of the disillusionment over the possibility of international cooperation, and from it many of the subsequent trade barriers sprang. We failed to enter the only organization which had any prospect of stabilizing political conditions peacefully. We insisted on war-debt payments and proceeded to make receiving them difficult. We raised our tariffs and insisted on greater exports. We endeavored to return to normalcy without an adequate contraction of war-expanded industries. We adopted an isolationist policy, and when aggression began in 1931, we declined to participate actively in checking it. The course of post-World War mistakes by major powers makes one suspect the validity of the statement that "the world gets the sort of government and economic conditions it deserves."

When one considers the activities of the League, the number of post-War conferences, the treaties signed, the volume of discussion and actions on international questions, the decade of the 'twenties appears to be one of great international cooperation. Yet, on the fundamental questions of finance, debts, trade barriers, economic readjustment, and economic development little more than the most opportunistic action was taken. At the World Economic Conference of 1927 an attempt was made to find ways of reversing the upward trend of trade barriers and self-sufficiency programs. Its recommendations were ignored, and instead, higher and more varied trade restrictions were adopted. The United States gave further impetus to this trend in 1930 by enacting the highest tariff in its history. By this time the disintegration of trade and the collapse of post-War prosperity were already under way. From this point on, only the formalities of coöperation were observed while each nation frantically adopted whatever protective monetary and trade policies seemed for the moment necessary. Britain found herself surrounded by trade barriers. She faced problems of balancing her international account and of insuring her economic requirements. As a result, she dropped her long-standing policy of free trade. And J. M. Keynes was able to shift his position to favor the new policy and add, "National self-sufficiency may be becoming a luxury which we can afford."

It was at least ten years too late to undertake seriously the reconstruction of a world economy of trade and peace. Nevertheless the United States launched its trade-agreement program of 1934. It looked like a modest and not too hopeful effort at the time. Since then it has stood out as the only significant attempt of a major nation to obtain freedom and equality of treatment in international trade.

Meanwhile, the aggression of "have not" nations demonstrated the dangers of another war, and drove nations, willingly or otherwise, to engage in economic preparation. The energies and resources of nations were diverted from peacetime trade to armaments; domestic industries were encouraged; unessential imports were restricted; treaties to insure necessary wartime supplies were sought; and entire economies were transferred from their place in what remained of world economy to the necessary function of self-preservation. Discrimination in favor of given nations, quota imports, bilateral trade balancing, international barter, exchange depreciation, clearing agreements, and exchange control became the spreading, if not the general, practice. Because such policies had effectively destroyed free international exchange for the nations adopting them, others were driven to adopt them. As a result, markets for exports were restricted, the foreign means of payment for necessary or desired imports became scarce, and such imports could no longer be relied upon.

If the unsatiated states have found it necessary to go to war for economic reasons of markets and resources, then those reasons are in large measure of their own making and follow from the commercial and foreign policies pursued. While all the great powers must share the blame for the entire course of events, including those which set the "have not" nations on the path of aggression, it is also clear that the motives in such aggression are not pure. Power imperialism on a different front and in modern guise is still with us.

The requirements of trade and peace.—Thus far the world has been ingenious in the technical conduct of trade, but it has failed to devise a political organization or an economic policy capable of achieving the advantages of trade without periodic conflict. One is inclined to wonder whether, in the future, world trade among politically independent states can and will continue in peace, without jeopardizing the independence of such states, or whether unity, and harmony between trade and peace, can be had only through political unity and the imposition of peace by centralized authority. If political unity is necessary, must we rely on imperialistic, military, political, and economic domination to produce it, or can we obtain the necessary degree of political unity through some form of voluntary coöperative action? These questions refer simultaneously to the future of peace, the future of national states, and the future of economic welfare.

Historical experience shows that, especially in periods of expansion, trade has furnished economic motives for imperialism and conflict. Merely extending the areas of economic contact will not insure peace. The resulting economic interdependence may enlarge the reasons for keeping peace, but exchange likewise increases the possible causes of friction. Aggressive trade promotion implies a disruption of vested interests and of established economic relations. Such practices of traders may drive a nation into imperialism and conflict, and drive others to resist.

Recent experience shows, too, that blocking economic intercourse at national boundaries will not insure peace. Such barriers to trade restrict economic opportunity, leave nations with an unbalanced distribution of resources and population, and promote the cry for markets, access to resources, and additional territory. The extension of economic and political control becomes almost inevitable. Thus, to improve the economic welfare of one group another is subjugated.

But between the policy of aggressive trade expansion, on the one hand, and economic isolation, on the other, is the policy of voluntary trade between nations respecting each other's independence. The greatest harmony between trade and peace can there be found, and it is this policy which has promoted most of the expansion of world trade and the greatest economic interdependence. The great industrial-commercial nations of the world typically have a larger stake in their trade with each other than with their colonies or the smaller powers. Through the intensification of trade they have become each other's best customers. The United Kingdom, Canada, Japan, France, and Germany are the leading customers of the United States, and these same states are among our leading sources of imports.

If world trade is to be conducted so as to promote peace rather than conflict, a free access to markets and resources is imperative. This implies equality of treatment toward all nations, and the absence of discrimination and coercion. It means, too, that to distribute fully the benefits of international specialization and trade, the economic significance of political boundaries must be minimized. But this cannot safely be done in a world endangered by war. Thus we return to the crucial issue on which the solution of the economic problem rests. It is the use of force as an instrument of national policy.

Until the post-World War years, there had been little question of the sovereign right or privilege of using force against an independent state. The policy of using it had for centuries produced a competitive race for power. Imperialistic expansion since the 16th century doubtless arose as much from the desire for what seemed like necessary power as from the desire for profits. It was the conjuncture of commercial and industrial expansion, on the one hand, and the rise of national states in a warlike world, on the other, which produced imperialism.

So long as force remains an instrument of international policy, power will be an object of national ambition, and conflict will result. National power is a relative matter. It must be achieved at the expense of other nations, whose power is thereby destroyed or weakened, relatively if not absolutely. Hence, the aspiration for power by one state produces competition for it among many. The competition magnifies conflicting interests and leads to war. The justification for war becomes the attainment or protection of national power; and power is necessary only because of the prospect of war itself.[5] Thus any threat to use force may produce a power economy and armed conflict. Remove the prospect of war and the nations of the world can proceed with their economic task by peaceful means. But neither limiting armaments by treaties which can be scrapped, nor controlling munitions makers, nor struggling for a balance of power, will eliminate the possibility and prospect of war. The only escape from this vicious circle is an unqualified renunciation of force as an instrument of international policy—a renunciation which the world will coöperatively make effective. Security against the possible use of external force would permit nations to adopt as their paramount aim the maximizing of economic and social welfare. International machinery for peacefully adjusting international disputes with reasonable speed and justice could then substitute rational behavior for force, and the pursuit of welfare could be undertaken on a world basis.

The chief problem of a peaceful world would be the one originally stated—to make the most of our scarce resources.

[5] R. G. Hawtrey, *Economic Aspects of Sovereignty* (London, Longmans, Green, 1930), pp. 26–27, 105–107.

This would involve either the shifting of population to resource areas, or the transport of resources and goods to the population areas. Because of the cultural differences and problems of assimilation, the former alternative holds little promise of success, except as used on an insignificantly small scale. On the other hand, the transfer of capital for economic development, the transfer of knowledge and technology, and the transfer of raw materials and goods hold large possibilities and constitute a feasible alternative. Such transfers could greatly improve the use of human and natural resources, with consequent improvements in economic welfare.

International development of this sort could not be obtained, however, without some relocation of economic activity so as to use each region for those industries which are best suited to it. The transition would benefit some localities immediately; it would, of course, temporarily or permanently injure others, but if the development should come gradually the pains could be lessened. Full development in any short period is neither necessary nor possible. Any trend toward such a world economy would improve economic welfare just as territorial specialization and trade has done in the past three hundred years. "We have come a long way already, many adjustments have been made, and to abandon world economy will cost at least as much in social upsets and political frictions as to develop it."[6]

Possibilities and prospects.—It is unnecessary to pursue further the advantages of a world economy. Instead we should

[6] Eugene Staley, *World Economy in Transition* (New York, Council on Foreign Relations, 1939), p. 85.

consider whether, in the light of current trends, a development in this direction is practicable or probable.

Three trends in particular have an important bearing on this question. One is the trend of technology; another is the trend of political development; and the third is the trend of warfare, which grows out of the first two.

In the technical field the trend has been, and continues to be, one which makes the world smaller and more interdependent. The reduction in time and cost of transportation and communication has reduced the world to but a fraction of its former size. While self-sufficiency programs in recent years have stimulated the discovery of substitutes for foreign goods, the results so far have been mainly to care for emergencies rather than permanently to reduce imports. Opposing this trend are the developments in modern industry and metallurgy, which require a greater variety of essential raw materials and alloys, many of which must be imported by every nation. The effect is to increase the geographical interdependence of economic activity in a world of shrinking distances. The consequences of spreading industrialization are not yet clear, but if past experience is any guide, the specialization will be such that trade between industrial nations will increase.

Our organizational and political ineptitude, on the other hand, has produced a conflict of technology and politics. In Eugene Staley's words, "while technology has been making for easier and larger movements of goods, capital, persons, and knowledge across boundaries, politics in recent years has seemed bent on erecting walls to resist these tendencies."[7] Out

----

[7] *Ibid.*, p. 51.

of this conflict, stability and peace can come only as these opposing forces are accommodated to each other. In recent years
the accommodation has been sought through the political disruption and diversion of trade. But what may be good politics
may be bad economics, and in the end we may expect economic pressure to drive men to make political adjustments.
Perhaps the accommodation will be painfully slow in coming;
perhaps world conquest will be the means; but the eventual
result seems now most likely to be some political federation of
semiautonomous states.

In considering the outcome of present trends, we may ask
whether the advantages of peaceful world trade and the costs
of modern war are not reaching levels which will make the
use of armed force unnecessary or unattractive. That the advantages of world trade are increasing is evidenced by its
growth in volume up to the recent depression and the multitude of restrictions which have been required to prevent
greater expansion. That war is becoming even more costly is
too apparent to require comment. The burden is heavier and
is borne by a vastly greater number of people than in earlier
years; whole populations of belligerent states are endangered,
and their economic welfare is reduced. But much of the cost
is also borne by neutrals, who must live in a warlike world
which periodically destroys its population and capital improvements, spreads privation and suffering, disarranges its
economy, and undermines its whole social structure for the
ultimate purpose of transferring the sovereignty over some
region and its population from one state to another. It is at
least conceivable that the growing costs of war may drive the

world to organize itself to suppress armed conflict between the nations. If this were done, the principal necessity and reason for politically erected barriers to trade would be removed. Thus a harmony between trade and peace might be achieved by removing the implement which nations now use for a multitude of goals including the acquisition of resources and trade. In the now fully occupied world, where imperialism can lead only to a redistribution of the spoils after costly conflict, the conditions for maintaining peace in the future seem more favorable than they have been heretofore, especially during the era of expansion since the great discoveries.

But we must accept the fact that today we live in a world still willing to pay the price which war entails. There is no assurance that in the near future man will succeed in making the necessary political accommodations to eliminate the use of force. There is ample basis, in both logic and experience, to indicate that autarchy in the present world of small independent states must inevitably lead to coercion and war. Possibly several large self-sufficient economic blocs, each carved out of present states by conquest and coercion, will be the result of autarchy. But the balance between such blocs based on power economics and conflicting ideologies cannot long endure.

In this warlike world of reality the greatest hope for future peace seems to lie in reversing the trend toward autarchy. To do this successfully the world must relax trade barriers, adjust trade practices of democratic and totalitarian states, reconstruct a stable international monetary mechanism, develop contractual loyalty, and create greater economic opportunity for "have not" nations. By thus restoring international trade, the economic ties between nations may be multiplied and some of the basic economic causes of conflict may be removed.

Today the American Trade Agreement Program is the only significant policy of a major nation devoted to a restoration of international intercourse and a world economy. It is a cautious, realistic program, founded on the principle of negotiated reductions in trade barriers and equality of treatment. Behind it is the recognition that the nations of the world must live together and trade together whether they like it or not. No nation can long pay the economic price of complete or nearly complete isolation. Behind this program is the conviction that a revival of international interdependence and trade is beneficial to the trading nations and especially desirable at this juncture in world affairs. It is hoped, too, that the program may lay the foundation for a restoration of sanity in international economic affairs and provide a basis for peace among nations. The greatest contribution of the program may yet prove to be that of keeping alive both the idea and the policy of international economic coöperation based on a voluntary liberalization of trade restrictions, equality of treatment, and mutual respect for the independence of nations.

In taking the larger view, this program inevitably runs counter to the self-interest of some groups while incidentally advancing the interests of others. It is intended to serve the interest of the nation as a whole and the world of which we are a part. But he who serves the national interest is like the economist who, in the words of Alfred Marshall, finds it extremely difficult to be a patriot and at the same time have the reputation for being one.

ORGANIZATION OR ANARCHY?

——

FREDERIC L. PAXSON

MARGARET BYRNE PROFESSOR OF UNITED STATES HISTORY
IN THE UNIVERSITY OF CALIFORNIA

Lecture delivered November 7, 1939

ORGANIZATION OR ANARCHY?

THE THEME assigned me is somewhat vague. The lecturers who have preceded me have dealt with specific problems, and each of them has had fairly well-defined boundaries within which to range. But my theme, "Organization or Anarchy?" covers the world, embraces all the hopes or fears of men, and calls for nicer balance, I fear, than I can hope to have. With much of the world at war, and with the rest of the world jittery lest it be drawn into war, it is hard to keep cool, and harder to be fair to facts. The voice of history, even when it deals with past events, is little more than a whisper; when it pretends to deal with the future it can rarely do little more than fool the listener. All that I may reasonably hope to do is to leave with you a warning which you may find it hard to take.

My title, I suspect, was not conceived without *Tendenz*. "Organization" and "anarchy" are not two terms of clear, recognized, and nontendential meaning. Their very selection implies a judgment by those who selected; and perhaps a measure of approval or disapproval. No one, I think, ever advocated organization in human affairs if he expected to take a loss from it. It follows from the choice of the word that those who picked it believed that through whatever it was that organization meant to them some good would be attained. This was not, perhaps, the sort of good to someone else with which those not sharing in it must put up; not the sort which, enjoyed by others, would of necessity react adversely upon those who promoted it; but a good which would induce a course of action generally harmonious with what they who propose it regard as useful to themselves, to their group in society, to their nation, or to the whole world.

Since all of us desire that which is useful to us, each from his own point of view, since all nations crave it, and since we live in a world of variant and often conflicting interests, it becomes obvious that in no two countries today could this word "organization" be discussed and yet retain identical connotations among those who spoke and those who listened. If we are to go far along the road which leads to prosperity for all, and permanent peace, and if others are to do the same, the many roads must lead to a single destination, from whatever corner of the world they come. That destination may not mean advantage to be enjoyed by blacks alone, or by the yellow races, or by the white. It cannot be one in which Aryans may not share, or non-Aryans.

To discuss this matter of organization upon any platform broader than that of any single nation, it must be discussed in terms of equal advantage to all. More than twenty years ago a great American statesman had this word in mind when he spoke of an association of nations. If he had spoken of an association of good nations, he would have fooled himself and vitiated his proposal. The world forgot; but he did not forget or overlook the fact that before any such structure could be built to stand, there must be agreement upon a condition precedent. This condition precedent he expressed in his phrase "peace without victory," a negative phrase meaning neither more nor less than that the world order must not be punitive to any vital interest. Like the fear of the Lord, his phrase was no more than the beginning of wisdom. Before Wilson or another could have turned the dream into reality, he must have gone far beyond mere negation; he must have been able to promise through organization positive advantages for all in excess of what any single group could hope to attain for itself through the use of its armed forces; and he must have been able to assure all that organization would not for any of them mean frustration or destruction. And so I shall ask you to look a little askance at this word "organization" as used in my title until it shall become clearer to us just whose organization it is that we discuss. We must purify it from any suspicion that it is our own organization which we offer as a panacea. It would be bad if, knowing that we were putting something over on the world, we should guarantee it as free from selfishness. It might be worse if, through loose thinking, we should let ourselves believe that we have a right to shape the world to our own image.

And "anarchy," too, appears to me to be highly tendential in its real meaning and its application here.

I began to hear about anarchists many years ago, when I was young; but it never occurred to me to go to the anarchist to find out whether what I heard was true. I have heard about them intermittently ever since, and I have begun to note that what I have heard has not been from the lips of avowed anarchists stating their beliefs and applying them to a world of fact. It has been, instead, from the lips, pens, typewriters, and headlines of those to whom the very word was offensive, who used it as a term of reproach and vilification, and who did not endanger the fervency of their emotions by exposing them to an accurate understanding of that which they bedeviled. I have a feeling, as I read my title, that anarchy is given me as alternative to organization, not as descriptive of a scheme of human order, but rather as suggestive of something which may, like the goblins, get us if we don't watch out.

By anarchy I suppose is meant world disorder resulting from international rivalry and self-help. The word carries a suggestion of bombs and destruction. It has an implication that the anarchist is an unsocial person or nation, creating disturbance for the sake of disturbance or of greed, and therefore a social or international nuisance to be abated by all right-thinking people. I have no confidence myself in anarchy as a rule for the happy life. But the philosophers who have elaborated it have not justified it because of its power to raise hell among the nations. They advocate it as a basis of what they say will be a happier and fairer peace than the world has known. They may, like other forecasters of Arcadia, be living in a world of iridescent dreams; but at least the dream has for them more charm than the world of reality from which it provides escape. Violence and combat, in their picture, become means, not ends; they appear to the proponents of anarchy to be the only means of jacking society out of its existing ruts so as to start it on a highway to the happy world in which, none being bad, and none being abused, there shall be no need of government by force.

I am driven to wonder if the anarchists are, after all, more violent or less reasonable than those who detest them, yet believe that after one more good war the evil nations may be driven from their evil practices and turned to walks of virtue.

The peace conference after the present world war, I suspect, will make the Paris Conference of 1919 look like a Sunday School picnic.

The words of my title need to be defined with care; but at their loosest they name a problem. We need to consider in cold blood the ways and means of attaining in the world—the real world, not one of fantasy—an equilibrium which may be generally fair. It must be so fair among social groups that its opponents will lack leverage to disturb it. It must be so considerate of reasonable requirements among nations that no nation will be able to convince itself that it can better its condition by the use of force. So long as men and nations differ in intelligence and in security, it is futile to expect unanimity. There can be unanimity only among the dead. The best which practical men can hope for is an equilibrium in which most people, most of the time, are too nearly content with what they have to be interested in wasteful violence for the purpose of acquiring what they have not. It must be an equilibrium implemented with administration which shall impartially interpret every existing rule until the rule shall be changed by orderly process. It must be an equilibrium, too, which shall not keep men and nations down, or keep them up. It must follow the maxim of Thomas Jefferson that governments derive "their just powers from the consent of the governed," and must accept his corollary that the people have an inalienable right "to alter or abolish" such governments as have failed to serve their need. But it must accept also his prudent proviso, less often quoted, "that governments long established should not be changed for light and transient causes."

Anarchy, in my title, is not that anarchy which philosophers and poets have dreamed about. It symbolizes, instead, violent, lawless, unilateral disturbance, which is offensive to the interests or sense of fairness of men whose feet are grounded within the boundaries of one of the competitive entities known as nations; nations in whose keeping, severally rather than collectively, rests the very existence of our world, let alone its peace.

But what I have to discuss is not peace and security, American style. It is rather peace and security as they may be capable of visualization and attainment upon a scale of global dimensions. Only the blind and the deaf today may forget that it takes two nations, at least, to make a peace. No more than those who wrote my title can I free myself from interests so vital to me that I cannot conceive as a good world one in which they are denied. But I should like to try to detach myself, and to take a look around, conscious always of the margin of error inherent in my point of view, but endeavoring to allow for it.

At the heart of my problem is the basic question, What have we to expect?

Have we, of necessity, to look ahead upon a world of conquest in which contesting programs will be equally right to their proponents, equally inadmissible to their opponents, and mutually contradictory? Is there no compromise possible that shall not mean conquest for some, and suicide or murder for others? Such a world would be, indeed, the world of biological life, in which the big fish feed upon the little fish, not violating as they feed their highest law of nature and of duty.

But the force which brought man down out of the trees, and made him man, rather than a beast, was his capacity and necessity to know some law broader than his own advantage or his immediate survival, and his willingness occasionally to postpone his own interest for the sake of a common good. We are all willing, too often, to let others sacrifice their own interest for the common good; the acid test is a willingness to impair our own. Nations and social classes are abstractions of the mind of man; and in their behavior they appear to roam in a twilight zone between the entities of growing life whose only duty is to survive and procreate, and the human souls whose cravings and imagination have led to organization and law. In many of their aspects governments can know no other law than that of the jungle; for no responsible leader dare let his people down for the benefit of an alien race. Yet all his people know, at the bottom of whatever it is we call a soul, that the logical end of jungle law for human entities is rivalry, combat, and destruction. We all know, too, when momentarily we think along the plane of universal good, that few laws last unless they are so generally useful that they substantially enforce themselves. We have little evidence in history of the capacity of individuals, or groups, or governments—dictators, parties, theocracies, or states—to lay down law for others and make the law as endurable for the others as it is for those who write it. We have little evidence, either, that majority groups working under the best of democratic principles, can often see the interests of minorities as clearly as they see the interest of those upon whose votes their power to rule depends. We have no right to the easy assumption that with democracy will come peace; there may come with it only its own kind of coercion and abuse if the party lines of the majority last too long. What we may say, with reasonable confidence, is that it is not safe to leave authority too long in the hands of any group or person, democracy or dictator, which has ceased to guide action by the desire of the governed.

We cannot look into this future with a comfortable assurance that we alone—or any we, wherever they may sit and hope—have found the one true goal and the one true method for attaining it. If we are ever to reach a world equilibrium which is tolerable to us, the price we must pay is that it shall be equally tolerable to those who, today, we fear may fight us, or whom, tomorrow, we fear we may be forced to fight. If we were merely beasts, we should merely fight. The strong would kill or enslave the weak; kill or be killed, and that would be the end of it. But since it is peace we wish, not mere survival, it must be a peace in which nothing vital to an alien or distrusted race is more denied to it than the indispensables are denied to us.

It is a large order which the human world gives to its thinkers, to devise and implement a world of peace. It is given at a moment when a quivering world has started upon another convulsion; started before its oldsters have forgotten the last convulsion; before its youngsters, disillusioned because the last great peace brought only discord, have tested their power to make a better peace. All that the world got out of the last World War was a concrete check upon what may have been an attempt to rule the world by force, and an Arcadian hint. A concrete check it was. It left a group of great but defeated nations prostrate and politically diseased. An Arcadian hint it was, necessary preliminary to action, but negative at best: the "peace without victory," little though it was, was too much to be attained. If one might hope that the full implications of Wilson's phrase could be achieved, even that Arcadian hint— that punishment must not be part of the superstructure of organized society—might provide a foundation for a better world. We believe, within the range of my voice, that democracy is a dependable procedure in the erection of the superstructure. But few of us can be certain how far we hold that belief because it merely profits us, and how far it represents a dispassionate diagnosis of the needs of all.

The antithesis suggested by my theme, "Organization or Anarchy?" contains a hint of courses along which to prospect the route to better things. There are not many principles of action which, pursued to the end, could conceivably produce a world in which each man's fate would depend largely upon his character and talents; in which the fate of every social group would rest upon an admittedly fair division of the products of industry and of the advantage coming from the possession of the products; in which the fate of every nation would be so nearly what the nation craves, and so similar to that of other nations, that men need not care whether they live in New York or Timbuctoo, in Danzig or in China, in some First Ward or in some Fifth; in which it would make little difference in the "pursuit of happiness" whether a man be as black as the ace of spades or as blond as the truest Nordic, or whether his religion were that of Christ or Buddha, of Moses or Karl Marx.

One of the conjectural principles is that which is suggested, not too accurately, by "anarchy" in my title; which means, I think, the route of empire built on force. The other, which appears to be the real meaning of "organization," is that of fair voluntary agreement. It is philosophically admissible that by either of these principles we might reach peace: something like a *pax romana,* or a *pax germanica,* or perhaps a *pax americana,* on the one hand, with superauthority laying down the law and administering its enforcement through an organization permeating the whole world, down to the last traffic cop. Or, by the voluntary organization of nations, it is conceivable that peace and law might come out of some federation of the world translating into action and control the temperate and informed will of the citizens of the world. Peace is not a condition in which there are no differences and no violations of law, but rather one in which the differences and violations are so unimportant as not to endanger security and order.

The imperial road toward peace, if not to it, is old stuff for the historian. More times than one may name, it has been traveled. It has been the route of ambition for its own advantage; of selfish national destiny, interpreted as sense of duty, glossed by the poet as a matter of the "white man's burden," and left at last to the historian to dig from its wreckage an account of its rise and fall. The route has been traveled in every stage of political transportation, always on legs until the mariners learned to build galleys and sail into the wind. Borne now on wheels, and through the air, driven by steam and gas, it is being traveled again. The power of our contemporary conqueror goes faster than the armies of Alexander could march to the confines of his world; or than the hordes of Genghis Khan could advance along the lines of grass. Always with a sharp cutting edge, death and duty have flourished on the frontiers. And in every stage of military science the better weapon has done quicker service than sound ideas. Ever avowing peace after conquest as the goal, empire has made war in the name of peace. And in every case on which the historical books have been closed, the final chapters on empire have described dual failure as the end. Dual failure, respecting the affair as a masked grab at power or as an honest drive at a secure world order. Historians have seen so many nations fall that they can hardly be surprised when any totters. Even their own may fall.

Because every effort at peace through power has thus far failed through toxins of its own creation, is no reason for dogmatic statement that peace may not be reached through extension of imperial power. It may only be that the true formula for survival has not yet been found. Perhaps some political genius, with power in his hand, may some day turn the trick. But there are certain conditions which have commonly attended the attempt of entrenched authority to stay entrenched which need to be examined before anyone in disinterest should lend his mind to the doctrine of imperial sway.

The advantages of such sway are obvious. They include simplicity of organization on a large scale, directness of operation from top to bottom, directness of promotion from bottom to top, decision and execution by the same hand. What seems to be lacking is what in absence of a better term may be called political virtue and human capacity. In all the cases which the

historian may examine, the tendency of imperial sway seems
to have been the interest of the emperor, whether he be man,
or class, or hierarchy. And when the ruler, satiated with
power, has gilded his greed with a professed concern for his
people, his mechanism for service has been clogged in the
gears by the less generous interests of those upon whose devoted diligence depends the success of any plan. These are not
satiated yet; and some of them seek the dictator's seat.

We have little evidence, I think, to indicate that men in
power can long as a group retain virtue. Even should they
retain virtue, we have as little evidence to indicate that when
the time comes to provide successors for the imperial architect
through whose rough skill the empire has been erected, the
successor will have the skill to carry on. Empire, in the hands
of the great emperor, drives on and dare not stop; in the hands
of lesser men it slumps. I am ready to concede the theoretical
possibility of a world empire so wise and good as to be fit to
last. But what I think I know of men induces profound doubt
about it. I am ready to believe that if the only chance of a good
world order lies in empire, there is no chance.

The antithesis to this imperialism, or to anarchy so long as
there shall be solvent rival powers in the field, is, I suppose,
some variety of coöperation or organization in which the un-
derlying principles of action are generated on some level of
the social order lower than that of the administering chief.
For the last quarter-century we have had held before our eyes
the antithesis of tyranny and democracy, and our half of the
world has been driven to a gilding of democracy by our conviction of the viciousness of tyranny. Only in the hither end

of the quarter-century have there been many, even in the other, totalitarian, half of the world, who have openly derided self-rule for its ineffectiveness, and openly lauded tyranny as a sound tool for public welfare. For the purpose of the argument, imperial structure stands in antithesis to organization voluntarily accepted by its component units. From a different angle, the antithesis looks like one of conflict between democratic and autocratic principles. And to some minds what is not of one of these is of the other, while the two together seem to cover and comprehend the whole range of possible action.

Be this as it may, the organization approach to peace is one which philosophically must be conceded as a possible route to the goal.

When, a few months after war broke out in 1914, the elder statesmen began to talk about the next world order, better of course, to be erected after the enemy to peace had been beaten down, a League to Enforce Peace made its appearance before the Western mind, and gained some converts on even the other side of the line of trenches. Its translation into an Association of Nations, designed to do things more positive than merely to enforce peace, came gradually. Yet it came rapidly enough to make for it a place among President Wilson's Fourteen Points. And to us of the United States it was so easy of intellectual acceptance that a little less rigidity in a President, or a few more votes in the Senate, might have landed the United States willingly in the League of Nations. ·

In most of the thinking about the League of Nations, as a type of world order built in denial of imperialism, there was undiscussed assumption that from such a League there would come an order acceptable to us and restrictive to those whom we distrusted. We failed to face the truth that if any order acceptable to us is to survive through its own virtue, it must be acceptable also to others whose immediate theories of life we may detest. There were few in 1919 to support the League, out of the millions who gave it praise, who supported it with their eyes open; who realized that among the prime functions of any League with a power to govern must be the duty often to say an emphatic No; or that the No might as easily cut across a cherished path of ours as across that of another nation. Such a No was suggested in 1931 when the World Court advised against an Austro-German customs union, and the political pressure against the countries which had signed it compelled them to abandon it.

To those who expect peace to be cut to our pattern, I have nothing to say. They are as the imperialists, proponents of power, and have on their hands only war. No one ever sincerely and intelligently accepted the principle of arbitration without also accepting the possibility of losing the suit before the arbitration court. None of those who accepted the League accepted it with full intelligence unless they accepted with it the clear chance of being voted down.

But the concept of a League made headway with Americans because it seemed to be an extension around the world of a principle which had managed, for more than a century, to maintain a moderate amount of peace within the United States. There would have been a less complete acceptance if Americans had had a better understanding of the causes of the Civil War, or a sufficient foreknowledge of the difficulties which were to develop in the United States in the decades after the World War. Before one assumes that our Federal solution is capable of generalization upon a world basis, in opposition to the imperial hypothesis, it is worth while to take a look at the American experience. Under our Constitution, the sesquicentennial of which has just been marked, has taken place the world's greatest experiment in federation.

Our experiment in federation has been a good experiment for us, but it may not be forerunner of a good world order. In the operation of any federation of the world, there must be, as there has been with us under the Constitution, three fields of possible action to test the intelligence and self-restraint of all who live within the federation or are charged with its administration. There must be, at the top, global problems, for which the solutions must be universal, expedient, and in the long run sound. The time and strength of the people are not to be wasted in short cuts to Utopia, which prove to be both long and vicious. Every subsection of a world state, in the arctic or in the tropics, will have an insurable interest in the rightness of general measures. Elementary prudence will restrict this field to those topics concerning which uniformity is vital. The vitality and the necessity of the general rule will test the self-restraint of those who like to do the thinking for their inferiors, and who wish by coercion either to rule the world or uplift it. Unless their rule be obvious to most of the people in most places, it will not work. There must be general rules in any world order; but in the hypothetical world state there is only pain ahead when measures shall be adopted, say, by a majority of little states like Luxemburg and Guatemala, or by pressure from a few great powers. Soundness is absolute requirement for the universal; but universal soundness is so hard to find that it will reduce the number of universal rules to the minimum.

The field for universal law is only one of the three fields of action, and is at the top. At the bottom lies a field within which world authority may intrude only at its peril.

I do not believe that it will ever be possible to regiment the world. There are too many kinds of people, too many ways of life; and all the kinds and all the ways are grounded in a historic past which makes them reasonable for those who like them. We know little about the differences in inherent value among the peoples of the world. We have, however, observed much concerning their preferences and habits. Some, from pride or possession, or from necessity, wear clothes; others, from convenience or lack of clothes, wear skin. Some rules of life, reasonable in industrial centers, would be nonsense at the edge of the jungle. The rules of manners, as of ethics or religion, useful to some peoples, would be only tyranny for others. Along this local and bottom level, law must be grounded in autonomy. The peoples concerned must remain free, not only from interference from above, but also from fear of such interference. They must be safeguarded in their right to be wrong—from the standpoint of others—if we are to have peace and they happiness. From another slant, there is always the bare chance that they may be right, and that what makes its appearance as a quaint local insanity may in time be turned to general use. The world cannot afford to deprive itself of the useful consequences of local trial and error.

In our American federation, which has worked well for us, we have had and are having trouble enough to limit the general rules to those matters which are general from necessity, and to leave to local preference all those matters which may be left to local preference without wrecking the whole nation. A Northern aversion to slavery, and a craving for a reform for which the South must pay, brought us once so near to shipwreck as to constitute a perpetual warning. A recent effort, springing from our rural regions and the South, to vote the Northern cities dry, became a near-warning, and did durable damage to our concept of the law. No other nation has had quite so much success as we in carrying general rules in one constitutional pocket and local rules in another, and in keeping them apart. It was our measure of success in doing this which contributed to an unreasoning American acceptance of the proposal for a world federation modeled on ours, as a means for peace. But we have seen sectional interests, based on local belief in injustice, able to invite us to shipwreck upon even our less than global scale. We have little reasoned right to expect that an inclusive world federation could be made to work as well as ours. If it were not wrecked by the little nations ganging up, it might as well be stifled by the great powers, sitting down. If there were built into it a complete power of veto by every part at will, there could be few world rules; if local predilection could be overruled by remote and alien votes, there could be no peace by general acceptance.

Lying between the top field of necessary universal rules, and the bottom field of equally necessary local autonomy, there lies the third field of possible action. Here, as the scale of federation should spread, we must expect difficulty to march with it. Here, we have had troubles of our own.

Between the matters of global interest at the top, and what, with a bad pun, may be called matters of glebal interest at the bottom, there lies and will always lie an intermediate field of possible governmental action. It will always be a zone of combat. We have action in two zones of this sort in the United States today, with one geographic region in each zone insisting that it proposes a matter requiring uniform action, and in each zone another geographic region declaring such action to be a form of tyranny.

In the zone of child-labor control a fight has gone on for a generation between those who believe that the curse of child labor may properly be exorcised by the votes of those who hate it, operating at long range upon communities in which it seems less bad than its alternative. Fighting in opposition, we have had those whom we may not certainly call uninterested in child welfare. They say they believe that labor laws must reflect the culture and standards of the communities in which they are to be enforced. There is no common ground. And whatever the merits of the controversy, the fight itself is the sort of fight that endangers happy federalism.

If child labor, as a middle zone, be not enough, there is the matter of lynching. Generally known as the Dyer Law or the Wagner Law, there is a well-debated proposal to give federal courts jurisdiction over the sort of mob violence known as lynching. The opponents of the proposed enactment do not ordinarily defend lynchings as a good; they object to the invasion of their states by federal law. Of the proponents of the law, too many for a happy solution reside in regions in which crimes giving rise to lynching rarely occur.

In this middle range of possible enactments, in which each new extension of general rules is and will remain highly controversial, are to be found the booster charges which may be expected to set off world explosions when a world federation shall make mistakes. They wrench our Federal Union. They may destroy a broader one. On a global scale, with ignorance and indifference to the local needs of remote peoples increasing with the square of the distance, they may not wrench, but wreck.

I cannot see in the principle of imperialism any chance for peace. Under it, the future looks to me like the past: a succession of near-empires, built on war, and to be scrapped before fulfillment. I cannot see in world federation, or in the superstate, however democratic may be the basis of individual and group participation, any promise of the wisdom which, providing right answers, will enact workable general rules. Nor can I see promise of a moderation in such a superstate that will leave to component parts full enough freedom to live their lives their own way until by the slow processes of education they may be ready for new rules, obvious enough to enforce themselves.

I cannot believe that a world ruled by force, whether the force be that of an emperor or of a democratic world parliament, can stand. Each, with its own peculiar incapacities, seems to me likely to die poisoned by its own toxins. And if these two possibilities for the future, all that are suggested by my title, were all there are, I should be obliged to turn com-

pletely pessimist, and see little more ahead than more of
jungle life. But I am no pessimist, and cannot bring myself
to believe the worst, even though I dare not hope that perfec-
tion is likely to be attained. I think I see a third possibility,
different from either alternative, one to which we owe much
of what we have today, one to which most of us will probably
continue to owe escape from cataclysm. It is not a formula
by which we and our friends are right and others always
wrong. It is not one under which our minds may formulate
the rules under which other peoples may be made to live. It
is not even one by which injustice may always be prevented
or redressed when it is committed against persons and nations
over whom our jurisdiction does not run. But it may be better
than the worst, even if it be less desirable than what we conceive to be the best.

It is the formula of the trader who pays when he must for
what he gets; who in a wholesome bargain pays always a little
more than he wants to pay, but always a little less than his
co-trader hopes to receive. This was called "balance of power"
once; and twenty years ago only the cynics admitted that they
still trusted to its protecting force. It is called, and with con-
tempt, "appeasement" now. But, after all, it is nearly all
there is to trust for those who have no jurisdiction within
which to compel others to do their will, and too little wisdom
to know what others ought to do. If half the world is ever to
fight to compel the other half to live the life it orders them
to live, refusing at the same time to permit the other half to
order its own internal life, there is nothing ahead but war.
But if those who go to market shall go willing to pay for what

they get, I cannot escape the belief that they will meet in the world's marketplace even hereditary enemies ready to bargain and to fulfill their contracts. No nation can well escape the possibility that events may compel it to maintain its existence by force; but no nation can honorably deny to other nations the similar right to live. Here lies the basis for the bargain.

Much of what we know as personal toleration grew up in the marketplaces of the world where merchants learned not to meddle with the irrelevant preferences of customers. It is possible that international toleration, and with it a measure of peace, may come from world bargains from which both sides shall make a profit. But whether or not a new balance of power shall establish peace, it seems clear that peace will not be attained by peoples endeavoring to impose their rule of life upon the affairs of others, or in any world in which huge and solvent groups live in the continuous belief of prejudice, discrimination, and persecution. So far as the little nations are concerned, and minority groups, I see no chance for peace save from toleration by their greater neighbors, a toleration which may expand if fear of hostile intervention shall shrink. But in the world of nature only those growing things survive which save themselves. Among the larger units of our life the inescapable craving for survival has led to bargaining in the past and will lead to bargaining in the future. The time may come when the doctrine of the contented customer will do more to make the world fit to live in than all the schemes of empire or of unified control, on any basis.